OVERCOMING
THE
Destiny Stealer

SUKAENA CALLANDER

This work is registered with the UK Copyright Service

S&S Global Services

Assisted by: Global Destiny Enterprise, LLC

Cover design by: Angela Mills Camper of Dezign Pro Printing & Graphics

First Printing, 2021

ISBN: 978-1-8383053-0-7

TESTIMONIALS

"The Devil is a liar." This is a popular phrase that I hear from Sukaena quite often, and she is right.

I have known Sukaena since 2008. She is very passionate about understanding the Scriptures and what God has made available for us, His children. This is very evident in personal conversations with her and reflected in this book.

Overcoming the Destiny Stealer is a tool that educates, edifies, and empowers people to know and overcome 'The Destiny Stealer." I find the personal stories very relatable and the Scriptures very insightful.

In addition, Sukaena was very upfront about her personal experiences, challenges, and struggles, which makes this book very down-to-earth and real.

Furthermore, the prayer and reflections in the book make it very practical. "Sukey's Overcomer Nine-Step Strategy" makes this book reference material to use repeatedly.

Get ready; this is not a "normal book." You will be shocked, inspired, entertained but much more importantly, transformed through this book.

You have a destiny to fulfil and you need to know "How to Overcome the Destiny Stealer"

David Adabale

Author, Speaker, Mentor

As a mother, reading my daughter Sukaena's struggles throughout her youth is very emotional and heartbreaking. However, there is overwhelming reassurance in her belief, faith, and confidence in Christ that with His strength, she can and will always overcome and defeat the destiny stealer. In Jesus' name. Amen.

Lorna Hanson

My name is Violah Mafuba, and l am a psychotherapist who has been part of Sukaena's journey. I witnessed the unmerited grace and the favour of God on her life. This book is a powerful tool and enlightenment for millions who have experienced abuse that such traumatic experiences can be overcome at some point at different stages of life. It is an informative tool to point us in the direction of seeking help and not to die in silence. There is help out there. Please don't struggle alone; seek help.

Violah Mafuba

Psychotherapist

It's a privilege and a great honour to have the opportunity to say a few words about this book *Overcoming the Destiny Stealer*. Having been part of Sukaena's journey, I am persuaded that every reader's life will be transformed without a shadow of doubt.

Sukaena Callander is not only an overcomer and an anointed powerful woman of God but she is also an agent of change.

This book is a powerful tool for professionals as it helps uncover all the symptoms and signs of the destiny stealer at work and how to deal with such. It also helps to release the next generation from the destiny stealer.

Overcoming the Destiny Stealer will transform your life. If you have ever been abused, molested, raped, rejected, or isolated, you need this book.

"My people are destroyed for lack of knowledge" (Hosea 4:6a, NKJV).

In the book, Sukaena has given us knowledge and also step-by-step tools to identify and expose the destiny stealer. Above all, she reveals how to overcome by the blood of the Lamb, the word of our testimony, and by putting on the full armour of God. She also gives the opportunity at the end of most chapters to:

a] Reflect

b] Pray

This book is a must-read. The issues addressed in *Overcoming the Destiny Stealer* are profound and priceless.

Evangelist Fikelephi Jackson

First off, let me start by saying "Wow."

I have had the privilege to get a glimpse of what Sukaena has allowed God to use her to write through this book *Overcoming the Destiny Stealer*.

The Scriptures say to whom much is given much is required. From the few chapters I have read, I can testify that Sukaena has been given much. The Enemy was surely out to steal her destiny, but thanks be to God who ALWAYS causes us to triumph in His name.

Blessings and congratulations on your new book. I cannot wait to read the rest.

Prophet Meltoria

Overcoming the Destiny Stealer by Sukaena Callander is such an eye-opening look at one of Satan's attacks on the body of Christ. Through her testimony of overcoming the tricks and schemes of the Enemy, she takes us on a journey of victory in difficult circumstances. Her scriptural teaching helps us to get biblical knowledge and spiritual strength to press through our own challenges until we expose demonic assignments and see victory in our own lives. A practical guide of divine steps that help us get free from the hands of the Enemy and stay free.

Yvette Benton From Gerald and Yvette ministries

GYM

ACKNOWLEDGMENTS

I thank the Lord Jesus Christ my Destiny Redeemer for carrying me through. You are mighty. Thank You for showing me Your greatness. It is so amazing I still cannot truly comprehend. I know You have me for eternity! Thank You, Lord!

My beloved husband, I love you and I'm forever yours. Thank you for allowing me to share our story and supporting me while I wrote. You are truly amazing. My PPK, I honour and cherish you!

Many thanks to my mother and sister who blessed me to ensure I finished! I love and appreciate you so much!

Thank you to my home church New Wine International, the senior pastors and leadership team—your support, teaching, and presence in my family's life have impacted our growth in Christ. We will continue to serve Christ through New Wine International!

Many thanks to Pastor Bev Tucker from Roscoe, Illinois for allowing me to reference her and her deliverance manual. Her book was one of the tools I used for self-deliverance.

Thank you to my mentors worldwide for pushing me when I didn't want to be pushed because you knew I had to finish!

Thanks to my prayer partners for being my Aaron and Hur supporting me to give birth to my assignment!

I appreciate and am eternally grateful to God for all of the family and friends I haven't mentioned. God bless you all.

I thank God for all of you who have enabled me in your own unique ways supporting me through this journey. I love all of you dearly. May God shower you with blessings for the commitment you have shown to get this assignment completed.

TABLE OF CONTENTS

INTRODUCTION

We have an enemy who is seeking to alter and destroy our destinies. The Bible describes this enemy *"as a roaring lion, walketh about, seeking whom he may devour"* (1 Peter 5:8, KJV). This enemy is searching with a vengeance for whom he can destroy. Ultimately, he wants to steal your destiny.

This enemy whom the Bible describes as the accuser of the brethren (Revelation 12:10) was himself a highly exalted angel known as Lucifer. His destiny was to stand in God's presence for all eternity. As Scripture puts it, he was a perfect definition of beauty (Ezekiel 28:11-15).

But that former beautiful angel called Lucifer lost his place of glory and was forcefully ejected from heaven (Luke 10:18, Isaiah 14:12-14). Today, he is known as the Devil, the dragon, Satan, the serpent, the father of lies, a thief, devourer. He is now identified with every vile and disdainful name (Revelation 2:20). Why? The answer is simple: pride, disobedience, and rebellion (Ezekiel 28:15, Isaiah 14:13, 14).

The Devil lost his destiny because he was proud. His pride led to disobedience to God and rebellion against heaven (Revelation 12:7). Of course, the Devil lost in his attempted rebellion. He also lost out on his destiny. Now, he is a loser who wants others to become losers like him. His central purpose is to make others lose their destinies just as he did.

With vengeance, he is searching for those he may devour. He wants your destiny. Yes, he does! He will do anything in his power to stop the plan of God for your life. He is cunning and watches our lives meticulously to separate us from our Father just as he has been separated. However,

1

our glorious God, Creator of heaven and the earth said in His Word *"Neither death nor life, neither angels nor demons, neither the present nor the future, nor any powers, neither height nor depth, nor anything else in all creation, will be able to separate us from the love of God that is in Christ Jesus our Lord"* (Romans 8:38-39, KJV).

God holds all power and glory in His hands. Through our Lord Jesus, He shares that power and glory with you. Hence, through His manifold grace, you can fulfil the purpose for which He has created you.

Over the years, I have experienced great agony not knowing who my enemy was. I gave him lots of access into my life and then wondered why I was going through so much hell. He was stealing my destiny. Nevertheless, in the process of overcoming, God taught me many strategies for taking my life back. Now, I will take you on a journey of how to overcome the destiny stealer and take your life back.

As I learned to obey God's every word and live in subjection to His will, I have experienced God's deliverance. He broke the power of darkness from my life, renewed my mind, healed my family, and restored my marriage. The journey was painful, and I wanted to give up many times, but it was worth it.

What are you dealing with in your life that has you bound? Are you giving the destiny stealer legal access to your bloodline? What spiritual doors are open? Are you living in sin and disobedience? Do you experience vicious cycles? If you answered yes to any of these questions, you are a candidate for the Enemy to steal your destiny.

Destiny is important to God. He created you for a specific purpose and has a plan to see you flourish in every area of your life. Our God does nothing without a purpose (Jeremiah 1:5). Therefore, you must ask yourself these questions: who do you serve? Who has power over your life? Is it the Devil or Jesus Christ? The Devil aims to replace God's destiny in our lives with anything that leads to death and destruction. He wants to make losers out of us. But God has predestined a particular path for our lives that leads to happiness, joy unspeakable, peace beyond understanding, prosperity, increase and fruitfulness, marital bliss, and above all, an inheritance incorruptible in heaven waiting for us.

Come on a journey with the Holy Spirit as we identify the destiny stealer in your life. Through the power of God break generational curses, remove shame from your story, and experience breakthrough from God's Word.

PART ONE

IDENTIFYING WHO THE DESTINY STEALER IS AND HOW HE OPERATES

CHAPTER ONE
THE DESTINY STEALER IN HISTORY OPERATING THROUGH DISOBEDIENCE, PRIDE, AND REBELLION

The Bible is filled with real-life stories to help us understand the different situations we encounter and how to actually overcome the destiny stealer. Before I share my journey, I want to speak to you about a man God was fond of. He calls him a man after His own heart (1 Samuel 13:14). His name is David. David was a king, handpicked and anointed by God for his destiny. David was a great man of faith and a worshipper. He was known to dance before the Lord and worship Him in spirit and in truth. God also had a covenant with David.

The destiny stealer recognized that David was a man of destiny, a man who was going places with God, so he presented him with the sin of pride, disobedience, and rebellion. However, in the Scriptures, we discover how David fell because of disobedience but was not overcome with the sin of pride or rebellion.

LET'S READ THE STORY OF DAVID AND BATHSHEBA:

It happened in the spring of the year, at the time when kings go out to battle, that David sent Joab and his servants with him, and all Israel; and they destroyed the people of Ammon and besieged

Rabbah. But David remained at Jerusalem. Then it happened one evening that David arose from his bed and walked on the roof of the king's house. And from the roof, he saw a woman bathing, and the woman was very beautiful to behold. So David sent and inquired about the woman. And someone said, "Is this not Bathsheba, the daughter of Eliam, the wife of Uriah the Hittite?" Then David sent messengers and took her, and she came to him, and he lay with her, for she was cleansed from her impurity; and she returned to her house. And the woman conceived; so she sent and told David, and said, "I am with child."

Then David sent to Joab, saying, "Send me Uriah the Hittite." And Joab sent Uriah to David. When Uriah had come to him, David asked how Joab was doing, and how the people were doing, and how the war prospered. And David said to Uriah, "Go down to your house and wash your feet." So Uriah departed from the king's house, and a gift of food from the king followed him. But Uriah slept at the door of the king's house with all the servants of his lord and did not go down to his house. So when they told David, saying, "Uriah did not go down to his house," David said to Uriah, "Did you not come from a journey? Why did you not go down to your house?"

And Uriah said to David, "The ark and Israel and Judah are dwelling in tents, and my lord Joab and the servants of my lord are encamped in the open fields. Shall I then go to my house to eat and drink, and to lie with my wife? As you live, and as your soul lives, I will not do this thing."

Then David said to Uriah, "Wait here today also, and tomorrow I will let you depart." So Uriah remained in Jerusalem that day and the next. Now when David called him, he ate and drank before him; and he made him drunk. And in the evening he went out to lie on his bed with the servants of his lord, but he did not go down to his house.

In the morning, it happened that David wrote a letter to Joab and sent it by the hand of Uriah. And he wrote in the letter, saying, "Set Uriah in the forefront of the hottest battle, and retreat from him, that he may be struck down and die." So it was, while Joab besieged the city, that he assigned Uriah to a place where he knew there were valiant men. Then the men of the city came out and fought with Joab. And some of the people of the servants of David fell, and Uriah the Hittite died also.

Then Joab sent and told David all the things concerning the war, and charged the messenger, saying, "When you have finished telling the matters of the war to the king, if it happens that the king's wrath rises, and he says to you: 'Why did you approach so near to the city when you fought? Did you not know that they would shoot from the wall? Who struck Abimelech, the son of Jerubbesheth? Was it not a woman who cast a piece of a millstone on him from the wall, so that he died in Thebez? Why did you go near the wall?'—then you shall say, 'Your servant Uriah the Hittite is dead also."

So the messenger went, and came and told David all that Joab had sent by him. And the messenger said to David, "Surely the men prevailed against us and came out to us in the field; then we drove them back as far as the entrance of the gate. The archers shot from the wall at your servants, and some of the king's servants are dead, and your servant Uriah the Hittite is dead also."

Then David said to the messenger, "Thus you shall say to Joab: 'Do not let this thing displease you, for the sword devours one as well as another. Strengthen your attack against the city, and overthrow it.' So encourage him." When the wife of Uriah heard that Uriah her husband was dead, she mourned for her husband. And when her mourning was over, David sent and brought her to his house, and she became his wife and bore him a son. But the thing that David had done displeased the Lord. (2 Samuel 11:1-28, NKJV)

Did you read it? David accepted what the Devil offered him and satisfied the desire of his flesh. He disobeyed the commandment of God and committed adultery. The destiny stealer used this strategy in an attempt to steal the glorious destiny of David.

The reality is that often, while walking with the Lord, we still need deliverance. The destiny stealer (temptation), generational curses (repeated patterns) and, the flesh (our own desires outside of the will of God), come into our lives as a result of sin and disobedience. In Psalm 51:5 (NKJV), David wrote by the Holy Spirit, *"Behold, I was brought forth in iniquity, And in sin, my mother conceived me."* David was a product of sin, something he inherited from being a child of his parents. From the moment he was born, David had the tendency to sin. He was a slave to sin as a result of his parents' sin until he eventually dealt with it.

Being a slave to sin meant that David had to grow and overcome his flesh. That is "self," the tendency to do your own thing, rather than be subject to God. This was what inspired the rebellion of Satan. The Scriptures call this "iniquity," self-ambition, self-will, self-desire, self-love, self-interest, self, self, self—all outside God's will and commandments.

This pushed David to the point that even though he knew who Bathsheba was, he went ahead and committed adultery with her, killed her husband, and married her.

David killed Bathsheba's husband to keep the baby a secret. David moved Bathsheba into his house and she became his wife. Wow, right! I know. The Lord held David accountable. He sent Nathan. Nathan released the word of the Lord to David.

> Then Nathan said to David, 'You are the man! This is what the Lord, the God of Israel, says: "I anointed you king over Israel, and I delivered you from the hand of Saul. I gave your master's house to you, and your master's wives into your arms. I gave you all Israel and Judah. And if all this had been too little, I would have given you even more. Why did you despise the word of the Lord by doing what is evil in his eyes? You struck down Uriah the Hittite with the sword and took his wife to be your own. You killed him with the sword of the Ammonites. Now, therefore, the sword shall never depart from your house, because you despised me and took the wife of Uriah the Hittite to be your own."

> 'This is what the Lord says: "Out of your own household I am going to bring calamity on you. Before your very eyes, I will take your wives and give them to one who is close to you, and he will

sleep with your wives in broad daylight. You did it in secret, but I will do this thing in broad daylight before all Israel."

Then David said to Nathan, 'I have sinned against the Lord.'

Nathan replied, 'The Lord has taken away your sin. You are not going to die. But because by doing this you have shown utter contempt for the Lord, the son born to you will die.

After Nathan had gone home, the Lord struck the child that Uriah's wife had borne to David, and he became ill. David pleaded with God for the child. He fasted and spent the nights lying in sackcloth on the ground. The elders of his household stood beside him to get him up from the ground, but he refused, and he would not eat any food with them. On the seventh day, the child died. David's attendants were afraid to tell him that the child was dead, for they thought, 'While the child was still living, he wouldn't listen to us when we spoke to him. How can we now tell him the child is dead? He may do something desperate.' (2 Samuel 12:7-18, NIVUK)

David's sin brought severe consequences as you read in the above Scripture passage. What David did secretly was exposed publicly, and the child born to him and Bathsheba died. After all God had done for David, can you imagine the grief and pain he experienced because he was only thinking about himself?

I'm sure he went through heaviness of heart, shame, and condemnation as he pleaded with God for mercy. However, the destiny stealer failed to destroy David because he did not give in to pride and rebellion. Once David realized he had sinned he repented. He quickly knelt down in prayer to beg God for mercy. David acknowledged his sin before the Lord and asked Him to cleanse him. *"He asked God to create in him a clean heart, O God, And renew a steadfast spirit within him"* (Psalm 51:10, NKJV). I am so glad God doesn't hold grudges. He forgives sin and moves on. The Enemy would have liked David to stay in his shame and guilt and alter his destiny, but our merciful God forgave his sins and gave him a second chance.

Sin always births consequences, even when we ask for forgiveness. Sometimes, our sins spill over to other generations as we see in the case of David and others: Eli (1 Samuel 2:30), Gehazi (2Kings 5:27), and Saul (1 Samuel 13:13,14). But also remember we have been redeemed from the curse of the law by the death of Jesus (Galatians 3:13).

The Lord is our Destiny Redeemer. Shortly after David's losses, God redeemed and restored him. God gave him another son named Solomon, and the Lord loved him (2 Samuel 12:24).

David was an overcomer. He conquered the destiny stealer. He prayed, fasted, anointed himself and worshipped the Lord. This story gives me great joy because, if David with his shortcomings can still be loved by God, there is hope for you and me. However, we must humble ourselves and seek God as David did. God will give you complete victory over the destiny stealer.

In order for the destiny stealer to succeed totally in a person's life. There must be a combination of factors: disobedience, being too proud to repent, and rebellion.

The Devil knows God always forgives as long as we are truly repentant and seek His forgiveness out of love. Therefore, the destiny stealer does not just want you to be disobedient, he also wants you to be too proud to repent and as a result, totally rebel against God.

Saul was the King of Israel before David, but God dethroned Saul. Like David, Saul sinned and disobeyed God. However, there was a major difference between Saul and David. David was not too proud to repent, and he was not rebellious. Saul, on the other hand, was too proud to acknowledge his sins. Instead, he tried to defend and justify his actions.

Let's read an account of this in 1 Samuel 13:8-14 (KJV):

Then he waited seven days, according to the time set by Samuel. But Samuel did not come to Gilgal; and the people were scattered from him. So Saul said, "Bring a burnt offering and peace offerings here to me." And he offered the burnt offering. Now it happened, as soon as he had finished presenting the burnt offering, that Samuel came; and Saul went out to meet him, that he might greet him.

And Samuel said, "What have you done?"

Saul said, "When I saw that the people were scattered from me, and that you did not come within the days appointed, and that the Philistines gathered together at Michmash, then I said, 'The Philistines will now come down on me at Gilgal, and I have not made supplication to the Lord.' Therefore, I felt compelled, and offered a burnt offering."

And Samuel said to Saul, "You have done foolishly. You have not kept the commandment of the Lord your God, which He commanded you. For now the Lord would have established your kingdom over Israel forever. But now your kingdom shall not continue. The Lord has sought for Himself a man after His own heart, and the Lord has commanded him to be commander over His people, because you have not kept what the Lord commanded you."

Whenever you discover you have walked in disobedience, your very first step is to kneel down in humility and ask God for forgiveness. The destiny stealer wants you to do the opposite. He encourages you to justify yourself and defend your actions, so he can keep you away from God. But God wants you to live in total submission to Him.

In another instance, Saul went as far as assaulting the prophet Samuel just after he (Saul) had disobeyed God. In his pride he was rebellious.

The Bible shows us this is 1 Samuel 15:1-3 (KJV):

Samuel also said unto Saul, The Lord sent me to anoint thee to be king over his people, over Israel: now therefore hearken thou unto the voice of the words of the Lord.

Thus, saith the Lord of hosts, I remember that which Amalek did to Israel, how he laid wait for him in the way, when he came up from Egypt.

Now go and smite Amalek, and utterly destroy all that they have, and spare them not; but slay both man and woman, infant and suckling, ox and sheep, camel and ass.

Here, God sent Saul the king on a simple mission to make war against the Amalekites and destroy *everything*, including the animals. However, when Saul went there, he did differently:

And Saul attacked the Amalekites, from Havilah all the way to Shur, which is east of Egypt. He also took Agag king of the Amalekites alive, and utterly destroyed all the people with the edge of the sword. But Saul and the people spared Agag and the best of the sheep, the oxen, the fatlings, the lambs, and all that was good, and were unwilling to utterly destroy them. But everything despised and worthless, that they utterly destroyed. (1 Samuel 15:7-9)

As we have read from the above passage of Scripture, Saul acted against God's commandment. Let's see how he reacted when confronted with his errors.

And Saul said unto Samuel, Yea, I have obeyed the voice of the Lord, and have gone the way which the Lord sent me, and have brought Agag the king of Amalek, and have utterly destroyed the Amalekites.

But the people took of the spoil, sheep and oxen, the chief of the things which should have been utterly destroyed, to sacrifice unto the Lord thy God in Gilgal.

And Samuel said, Hath the Lord as great delight in burnt offerings and sacrifices, as in obeying the voice of the Lord? Behold, to obey is better than sacrifice, and to hearken than the fat of rams.

For rebellion is as the sin of witchcraft, and stubbornness is as iniquity and idolatry. Because thou hast rejected the word of the Lord, he hath also rejected thee from being king. (1 Samuel 15:21-23, KJV)

Again, Saul tries to justify his actions. He said he brought the best animals from the land to sacrifice to God. But God is not interested in sacrifices; He prefers obedience.

Do you find yourself being ashamed to admit your faults, even though you know you were disobedient? Do not be too proud to say I am wrong and beg for forgiveness; otherwise, the Devil will use this pride to create a gulf between you and God. *"God resisteth the proud, but giveth grace unto the humble"* (James 4:6, KJV)

Saul's pride pushed him until he assaulted the prophet Samuel and went on to murder other prophets of God. At the end of his life, after the Devil finally stole his destiny, Saul resorted to witchcraft—a sorry case indeed!

Saul's life story is a perfect example of the consequences of being too proud to acknowledge our sins and repent. If you have sinned, repent and seek God early while He can be found. This way, the destiny stealer will not be able to steal and destroy your life.

Will you be a man or woman after God's own heart? The choice is yours!

CHAPTER TWO
THE DESTINY STEALER IN HISTORY OPERATING THROUGH DISTRACTION AND REPETITION OF SAME TACTICS

We all have a common enemy: Satan, also known as the Devil, Lucifer, or the Fallen One. We now identify him as the destiny stealer. The destiny stealer is hateful. He detests the children of God, born again Christians, those who love the kingdom of God and follow Christ and His every word. I am a Christ-follower, so I know I am hated by Satan, and he has a plan to destroy me. *"The thief does not come except to steal, kill, and destroy. I have come that they may have life and that they may have it more abundantly"* (John 10:10, NKJV). The Enemy's desire on every level is to steal your destiny and mine. However, the good news is that Christ died so we may have life. Therefore, no matter what stunts the Enemy pulls, God is present.

John 10:10 has brought me a lot of comfort throughout my life. I have experienced the Devil's attempts to kill, deceive, and destroy me. Nevertheless, I am reassured in my faith because Christ loves me with unconditional love, and He has kept me through it all.

I have also learned to discern the tricks of the Enemy and why he continues to come after my bloodline. God removed the scales from my eyes; now, I can recognize the destiny stealer's tactics! Before I was even born, the Fallen One has tried to steal from me. He tried to take my destiny by making me feel illegitimate and rubbing me with shame. He then tried to use the spirit of rejection to overwhelm me. However, even though I battled with these things, God gave me the victory.

No New Tricks

The destiny stealer is never tired and will use the same tricks repeatedly. He has no new tricks. He uses the same old methods to cause us to fall each time. There is nothing new under the sun. Satan just keeps repeating the tactics that caused him to fall over and over again. He masquerades them to look different and modern. They are all the same old, serpent tactics. *"The thing that hath been, it is that which shall be; and that which is done is that which shall be done: and there is no new thing under the sun. Is there anything whereof it may be said, See, this is new? It hath been already of old time, which was before us"* (Ecclesiastes 1:9-10, KJV).

From the foundation of the world, Satan has been trying to destroy the human race. He deceived Adam and altered his destiny by using the closest person to him to lure him into disobedience. The Enemy used Eve to distract Adam. Hence, he forgot what God instructed him to do. The primary aim of the Devil was to steal Adam's destiny through disobedience to God. To get Adam there, Satan needed a good distraction. And he found one. Adam got distracted and Eve was deceived. Through her, Adam was also deceived. When the deceiver came on the scene, Adam's focus moved from God's attention to the Devil's intention. As I mentioned before, he comes to steal, kill, and destroy (John 10:10, KJV).

Sadly, Adam's distraction allowed the destiny stealer to come in and deceive Eve. While the cunning serpent tricked Eve, Adam was not present. Maybe if he were, he would have defended Eve from the snake and stopped the situation. However, by the time he arrived, man's destiny was rewritten. The destiny stealer continues to do the exact thing. He causes us to be absent when we should be present. He causes us to be callous and unintentional about the will of God.

In times like these, we are distracted by bad situations, hurt, disappointments, and pain of all sorts that shift our eyes off our God-given purpose. And in this vulnerable state, we then do things that allow Satan to steal our destinies. The eating of the fruit caused humanity's entire history, future, and destiny to change. But God in His infinite love reversed the situation and caused it to work out for our good, confirming His Word, which says *"And we know that God causes everything to work together for the good of those who love God and are called according to his purpose for them"* (Romans 8:28, NLT).

Another example of the Devil's repetition of tactics using distraction is in the story of Abraham and Sarah. The Devil used the same schemes with Abraham and Sarah as he did with Adam and Eve,

God had made a promise to Abraham that he would give him a son and his children would be as much as the stars in the skies. Abraham believed God and so did his wife. However, as life went by, and they both grew older, Sarah was overcome by fear and insecurity. Naturally, she felt she could no longer bear children, so Abraham might die without an heir. This was a big concern for her.

Sarah became consumed by this thought and gradually, she was distracted from God's promise, faithfulness, and ability to perform the impossible. In her vulnerable state, the Enemy seized the perfect opportunity to slip an unpleasant thought into her head.

> *Now Sarai Abram's wife bare him no children: and she had an handmaid, an Egyptian, whose name was Hagar.*
>
> *And Sarai said unto Abram, Behold now, the Lord hath restrained me from bearing: I pray thee, go in unto my maid; it may be that I may obtain children by her. And Abram hearkened to the voice of Sarai.*
>
> *And Sarai Abram's wife took Hagar, her maid the Egyptian, after Abram had dwelt ten years in the land of Canaan and gave her to her husband Abram to be his wife.* (Genesis 16:1-3, KJV)

Sarah gave her maid to Abraham as a mistress—a terrible mistake, indeed. At the time, Abraham himself was distracted. If not, he would have convinced his wife of God's faithfulness and their reasons to wait.

The Devil threw the smokescreen of distraction both ways—at Sarah and Abraham. Whilst their eyes were away from God's promises, the destiny stealer tricked them with lies that brought much sorrow, which extends to all Christians today. Hagar, (the maidservant Sarah persuaded Abraham to have a child with) despised and disrespected Sarah after she became pregnant. Hagar and Ishmael caused great heaviness to Abraham as he had to let them go.

The destiny stealer has not stopped using distractions. He still does today. Hence, the Bible warns us not to lean on our own understanding but trust in the Lord always (Proverbs 3:5-6). You should also not be carried away by what seems right and moral to you: *"There is a way which seemeth right unto a man, but the end thereof are the ways of death"* (Proverbs 14:12).

Gideon was a great warrior and servant of God. After defeating the Midianite army with just 300 men, he was tempted by the destiny stealer who wanted to affect his destiny. After Gideon's miraculous victory, the children of Israel asked him to be their king. Of course, Gideon declined. He told them only God could be their king. The Enemy was using the people to distract Gideon. The destiny stealer knew Gideon would not try to take over God's authority to be king over the Israelites. At that time, the Israelites had no earthly king. God was their king (1 Samuel 8:7).

This request was the distraction that caused Gideon to make a terrible mistake, which affected his destiny. Let's read from Judges 8:22-26 (GNT):

> *After that, the Israelites said to Gideon, "Be our ruler—you and your descendants after you. You have saved us from the Midianites."*

Gideon answered, "I will not be your ruler, nor will my son. The Lord will be your ruler." But he went on to say, "Let me ask one thing of you. Every one of you give me the earrings you took." (The Midianites, like other desert people, wore gold earrings.)

The people answered, "We'll be glad to give them to you." They spread out a cloth, and everyone put on it the earrings that he had taken. The gold earrings that Gideon got weighed over forty pounds, and this did not include the ornaments, necklaces, and purple clothes that the kings of Midian wore, nor the collars that were around the necks of their camels. Gideon made an idol from the gold and put it in his hometown, Ophrah. All the Israelites abandoned God and went there to worship the idol. It was a trap for Gideon and his family.

Gideon declined to be king. That was the right decision. However, he erred by making an idol for the people. Watch out closely for the Enemy; he still uses the strategy of distraction today.

Identifying the destiny stealer in your life is paramount. It enables you to live and walk in your divine purpose. It is very important to recognize the Enemy working in your life now and before you were born. Once you have identified him, you can eliminate and permanently shut him out of your life for good. Being delivered and overcoming the Enemy is a way of life. You must defeat Satan daily. Just as we bathe daily to maintain our cleanliness, we must seek deliverance daily to remain overcomers. The destiny stealer always tries to steal your destiny. *"Stay alert! Watch out for your vicious enemy, the devil. He prowls around like a roaring lion, looking for someone to devour"* (1 Peter 5:8, NLT).

CHAPTER THREE
OTHER NOTABLE TACTICS OF THE
DESTINY STEALER

The Devil wants your destiny and mine too. To help you better understand this, I will share my life's journey with you showing how the Enemy used my childhood to alter my adulthood. Although my childhood had pleasant memories, there were some unpleasant ones as well. Purposeful and deliberate seeds were sown into my life as a child and were watered as I grew into adulthood. I pray and encourage all parents and those who hope to be parents one day, please get to know the issues in your spouse's bloodline, past, and present. Research and ask questions about your own history. In doing so, you will identify historical or generational issues you and your children need deliverance from. Having this knowledge equips you to pray and cancel all assignments of the Enemy in your family through the blood of Jesus. This is even more helpful when you pray before having children or even getting married.

1. STRONGHOLDS: (WHAT YOU SEE)

PINK PANTHER

My earliest childhood memory is as a four-year-old watching a Pink Panther cartoon. I don't enjoy watching this particular cartoon with my children or anybody else for that matter because it brings back memories of my first sexual incident. I was unaware at the time of exactly what was happening to me. I thought it was a game. I tormented myself for years because I thought these feelings were normal. I was disgusted with myself as the sensation felt nice or what I thought was nice. Here is some science: our genitalia have the same sensitivity level from the moment we are born.

You may have heard children say that their private area tickles or is sensitive. So if a four-year-old's private parts are stimulated, they will start to crave physical touch. Oh, how the Devil is a liar! It wasn't an adult who began my sordid journey into sexual immorality; it was a person not much older than me who I believe was misguided into inappropriate sexual behaviors.

My body was conditioned and stimulated to have sexual feelings from an early age, and I didn't realise it. This incident wasn't predatory, and I don't believe it was deliberate abuse or harm. The destiny stealer was trying to rob me of my youth and purity. He may have tainted me and thwarted my views in specific areas, especially sex, but God had a plan.

This incident was the beginning of a roller-coaster journey into sexual abuse and opened the door for the spirit of lust and perversion. I did not realise or understand that this awakening of sexual feelings at only four years old was wrong. The sensation stuck with me.

What we see and are exposed to shape our perspectives of life; this is even more so for children who cannot identify good from bad. The destiny stealer is very aware of this and uses it as a tactic to corrupt the minds of young children. He uses the media to sow seeds of destruction that turn kids away from part of their destiny. This eventually becomes a stronghold and if not addressed in time with prayer and the Word of God may lead to irreversible mistakes.

2. IDOLS (OBJECTS): WHAT WE TOUCH

MY NUNU (TEDDY BEAR)

I am the second child in my immediate family and the first girl of five siblings I grew up with. At a young age, I had to take on a lot of responsibility, which I am truly grateful for. I have also taught my children to be responsible. Responsibility develops independence and maturity. I was a happy child with a confident disposition despite what I was going through. When the unsettling moments arose, I would continue, as usual, without realising they were not everyday occurrences of family life. During my childhood, I gained a good understanding of my family dynamics. In our house, lots of squabbling, arguments, and fighting between siblings took place. My brother, who is next in line to me, bickered a lot. He was only 2 1/2 years younger than me and there was what I would call a power struggle going on between us. On reflection, I always felt I had to discipline him. I used a bandana as a wapper (a hitting weapon). I would smack him with it when he didn't cooperate and do what I requested. He didn't like it, and in return, he would tease me mercilessly and hide my comforter all the time. My Nunu, my beloved comforter was extremely important to me, so hiding it would generate some over-the-top behaviour from me.

As a toddler between the ages of 2, 3, and 4, I always had Nunu with me. I hated it being washed or tampered with by anyone. What started out being an average size blanket for a bed was cut up into pieces and given to me by my mum simultaneously. As she washed one, she would have a clean piece to give me. I tried my best to hide my Nunu so it couldn't be washed, but Mum insisted on doing so. I resented it. My Nunu, which means teddy bear in French, comforted me. I smelt it, cuddled it, and loved it. I slept with it mostly as a child. I enjoyed sitting quietly with it. Everywhere I lay my head, it was there. This "thing" became a massive part of my life, even my marriage. I believed with my whole heart I would not sleep well if I didn't have it. In the early days of motherhood, I realised that using it in the day while on the sofa would make me fall asleep. So I quickly learnt that to fulfil my role as a mother excellently and effectively I had to stop that. I would leave it in my bedroom and only use it at night.

Naively, I even put it before my beloved husband. From time to time, he would ask, "Who do you love more, me or Nunu?" I would become defensive over this statement. How can you compare yourself to a piece of cloth? I had no clue that I was making this dirty pillowcase an idol and destructively, a soul tie.

Idolatry is seeking security and comfort from something or someone in replacement of God. It can be a thing like my Nunu or a person. We do this by seeking their approval above God's Word and before we seek God. Soul ties are created to things when we seek and need them more than God. Soul ties can manifest from idolatry. You can be soul tied, not only to people but also to things. Soul ties happen

28

when your spirit becomes entwined with something. The "something" doesn't always look or feel bad; however, and it is identifiable by what it produces. For example, my Nunu felt good and comforted me, but it became unhealthy because I relied on it more than God. I had made it an idol. That's when the soul tie traps and stops you from seeing this is the destiny stealer's work. He snares you and has you gripped in idolatry.

I loved this piece of blanket so much it knitted together with my soul. I became so dependent on it that if I couldn't get it, I would behave badly. As I said before, I would do all I could to stop it from being washed. If my mum washed it, she would say it got wet or caught in the wash to soothe me and reduce my tantrums. I liked the unclean smell of my Nunu. Can you imagine that? This is key to what the Devil does to us. He makes us believe that the worse or the dirtiest things are good. He made me believe my dirty comforter was a necessity! I thank God my mum saw it fit to wash it regularly! At 14, my mum took away the blanket and during that entire season, I did not sleep well.

3. IDOLS (PERSONS)

R & B STARS

Without my Nunu, I developed a massive crush on some R&B stars of the time. To sleep well, I used to pray to dream about them, and I did. The more I dreamt about them, the more I listened to the music. I wanted to dream of being intimate with them. I lacked something that I thought was my Nunu, which then turned into a want and a personal desire. Then *boom,* I had a spiritual husband! Selah! Ignorance is truly not bliss!

Another dirty trick of the destiny stealer is to connect us with things that make us feel good in our flesh but are wrong for our spirits. The destiny stealer manifested a spiritual husband through these intimate dreams and the molestation I had gone through as a child. It impacted my desire to dream about this man. Dreaming of being intimate with people is not a good sign. Dreaming you are having sex with someone is the incubus and succubus spirit manifesting in your dreams. If you are having dreams of being intimate with people, upon awakening, you must renounce and cancel every spirit of incubus and succubus and plead the blood of Jesus over your life. Understand that these spirits are trying to steal your marriage, your natural husband, and your womb! This is the Enemy at his finest but remember your Daddy is Jesus Christ. These spirits cannot stay if you rebuke, cancel, and renounce them. They only remain if legal access is given to them; as soon as you deny them access, they must leave.

Sometimes we may need to take extra precautions to get rid of deep ancestral strongholds by prayer and fasting. Sin can be deep-rooted; therefore, we must take different actions to get the deliverance.

> *Then, I set my face toward the Lord God to make requests by prayer and supplications, with fasting, sackcloth, and ashes. And I prayed to the LORD my God, and made confession, and said, "O Lord, great and awesome God, who keeps His covenant and*

mercy with those who love Him, and with those who keep His commandments, we have sinned and committed iniquity, we have done wickedly and rebelled, even by departing from Your precepts and Your judgments (Daniel 9:3-5, NKJV).

By accident, I discovered that a dirty pillowcase produced a similar smell as my Nunu, so I tried to keep one and make it my Nunu. However, one particular morning I walked into the bathroom just to find my mum putting the pillowcase in a bucket of soapy, stain-remover water. I confronted her and said, "Mum, I saw you just drop it in the water." My mum promptly denied this. "I said, "No, mum, I caught you!"

She said, "Well, you can't use this particular pillowcase as a Nunu. My mum then found a pillowcase that was grey and black with flowers. She allowed me to use this pillowcase as it wasn't a part of a set anymore. My comforter, idol, and soul ties were back!

I was out of the dream phase—so I thought. But not before one very horrible dream that occurred. I was about 14 years old, and I felt a massive, cold, black snake enter my bed from the side, next to the wall. I was awakened immediately by a bite on my thigh. I ran terrified for my life out of my room to my mum. Out of breath, I tried explaining to her a snake had bitten my thigh. The exact spot where I was bitten had two puncture holes in my leg matching a snake bite with a blister. I was terrified and badly shaken. My mum immediately prayed. She knew snake bites meant bad business.

I thought my mum was unaware of the sexual perversion in my life at the time. I was wrong. She was unaware of the molestation but aware and not pleased about my unhealthy desire for boys and attraction to R&B stars. Nevertheless, it did not come across as anything other than normal teenage behaviour. The blister on my leg grew to the size of an old ten-pence piece. My mum gave me antihistamines to stop the itchy crawling sensation. That evening when I bathed, the blister burst and was oozing pus. It eventually healed after a couple of weeks; however, I was quite scared to sleep in my room for a few days. I slept with my mum often. Now that Nunu was back, I relied on it heavily. Soon after Nunu returned, the sexual dreams and their frequency reduced.

4. GOD AND GOD ALONE

MY NUNU OR GOD

Once I left home, I had the freedom to do as I pleased with my Nunu. Can you guess what stopped happening? Yes, I never washed it. The only time I did was when my beloved husband and I got married. So right before my wedding day in 2005, I washed my Nunu. I relented as I knew he struggled with the notion that I put Nunu first, so I thought I had better wash it for peace sake. I finally got rid of my Nunu in April 2018 during my marriage crisis. The Lord told me I needed to rely on Him only. I needed to depend and trust Him in all things, including comforting me, and the ability to sleep without Nunu.

God also said to me, "I am a jealous God." At this time, I didn't understand, but when I read the Scriptures below, I got a clearer picture of why it is important not to make an idol of anything. I must love nothing more than our Father God! I was at a marriage conference in California at the time and received some incredible deliverance. This was the start of my deliverance from my childhood trauma. I still needed to be delivered from much more. After this time, I decided to get rid of my comforter, my Nunu. I took a photo of it that I eventually deleted and threw it into a hotel room's trash. I am glad I left it there as a way of knowing there was no retrieving it. I catch myself giggling in awe; I don't even miss it.

"But Joshua said to the people, "You cannot serve the LORD, for He is a holy God. He is a jealous God; He will not forgive your transgressions nor your sins. If you forsake the LORD and serve foreign gods, then He will turn and do you harm and consume you, after He has done you good" (Joshua 24:19-20, NKJV).

"God is jealous, and the LORD avenges; The LORD avenges and is furious. The LORD will take vengeance on His adversaries, And He reserves wrath for His enemies" (Nahum 1:2, NKJV).

5. WRONG EXPOSURES

MOLESTATION

"Do not be misled: "Bad company corrupts good character" (1 Corinthians 15:33, NLT).

No matter how good and pure you are, if you are constantly mixing with people who are living in sin, it won't take long before you join them. The Devil understands this, and he uses this strategy to affect lots of people before they even realise it. The problem of my molestation can be linked directly to being with the wrong people. I was exposed to people who took advantage of my naivete, rather than people who would build me up in the knowledge of God or help me understand what I was going through. The destiny stealer exposes you to people who will help destroy your destiny rather than build it. This is one of his weapons for stealing people's destiny. He used this tool on me as a child by pushing me toward people who just wanted to use and take advantage of me. But God always intervened to save my destiny.

The destiny stealer puts you in the wrong place, at the wrong time, with the wrong people, and the wrong attitude. This makes it impossible for you to get anything good out of the good life God has planned for you. The Devil used this weapon of wrong exposures to expose me to sexual abuse.

The hidden secret side of my childhood was the extent of sexual abuse I was experiencing. It made me promiscuous and triggered me to leave home at 16, which was way too early. I didn't realise God was protecting me from the destiny stealer. What could have carried on into my adult life didn't; the abuse stopped when I left home and moved out of the area.

The "abuse," so to speak, began in my ninth year. This year had many unusual events; sadly, the beginning of my molestation journey was one of them. I was interfered with prior, but I didn't have any predatory grooming and full penetrative sex until this time; it also coincided with when I started to menstruate. I started my period at nine years old and never got pregnant during this time of abuse, so I believed I was infertile. This was a lie from the pit of hell.

My brothers and I were taken out on weekends by this abuser. On the first occasion, he got my brothers out of the van. They were typical young boys playing football, and I was left there alone with him. He began to touch me inappropriately. I remember looking in this man's face and saying to him, "I know what you're trying to do with me." He looked at me quite puzzled with a mix of terror. We didn't see him again for a year. He later told me that he waited to hear if I was going to report him. I now wish I did. He stayed away to make sure it was okay for him to return.

The Devil operates the same way with his plots to harm us. He takes the opportune moment to plant seeds and water them. He is cunning and subtle and waits for the most powerful moment. The Enemy cleverly allowed the abuser to return. But nothing is new to God, and He warns us about the Enemy's tricks. *"Stay alert! Watch out for your great enemy, the devil. He prowls around like a roaring lion, looking for someone to devour"* (1 Peter 5:8, NLT).

The destiny stealer was trying to manipulate and silence me through this abuser. This man would come every Saturday and take us to the sweet shop. He used food, chocolates, and sweets as a silencer. I also developed a food craving and an addiction to whole nut chocolate. Whole nut chocolate is milk chocolate with hazelnuts. My mum would buy it and give me a piece of the big family bar at home. However, when this man took us out, I could have a whole chocolate bar for myself and anything else I wanted. Nothing was off-limits. He did the same for my brothers. My brothers and I were being groomed and manipulated by this man. Gluttony was introduced as I had to finish my chocolate before I got home. I could bring small things home or a little chocolate but not all. If I did, he would make me say he bought it for all of us. Tragically, he groomed me to make me believe this was normal. I would look forward to the chocolate and all the attention he gave me. Little did I know that the Enemy was trying to steal my destiny, purity, life, and womb.

Another way this man got me to be quiet was by using fear. I was quite an outspoken young girl, so family and friends may ask how come I didn't speak out. Firstly, I believed everyone had this secret and secondly, I was petrified. One day, he was able to take me out by himself. I think he took us to see his wife. Whilst the boys were occupied, he carried me to the cemetery. Once there, he showed me a fresh grave of a young girl he had previously molested. She had died as a child. At the time, I had no clue why he did that. I just said okay. I didn't even ask how she died. I just knew it was recent. As an adult, I reflected on some of the things he did to me. I now realise and understand that these were all strategic forms of grooming and instilling fear in me. Sadly, it worked, and I never spoke out. I believed if I had spoken out, I would end up in the cemetery. I didn't want to end up in a grave, so I always cooperated. I was being groomed on how to conduct myself with a man. This early sexualisation made me act inappropriately.

I started to misbehave at school. As a matter of fact, if I had been behaving like that in 2020, we would have all been removed from our family home and placed in the care of social services. In the early 80s and 90s, there was still a lot of naivete about sexual abuse; it was swept under the carpet.

At school, I went around saying I was pregnant. I can remember one of the dinner ladies (someone who supervised the children after lunch in the playground) who was quite old and slightly racist. She thought I was a little bit precocious and over-the-top. So when I began saying on the playground I was pregnant, it wasn't taken seriously. I was trying to speak out about my abuse but because of the times, my claims of being pregnant were ignored.

I began swimming lessons at my local swimming club, and the manager was amiable. I would say hi, converse, and debate with this man. In long conversations with him, he revealed that he had just married a Black lady. He was Caucasian. He would talk about his wife and how he was trying to have children with her. He revealed that he couldn't because he had a vasectomy. Being a child, I had no idea what that was. I asked, and he explained. I would have these long conversations with the manager twice a week. I'm sure you're reading this and wondering where my parents were through all of this. Our parents would drop us off and come and pick us up when it was time.

The destiny stealer had a plan to destroy my integrity and belief. The Enemy wanted me to believe that I deserved the years of abuse and it was my fault that all these things took place. One day, I was playing in the office and bent down to tie my shoelace. As I got up, I saw a bulge in the manager's pants. I got off the floor and grabbed his pants. I was in shock for a moment, and there was an uncomfortable pause. The manager said, "You can do it again if you like." I was crying out for help from my other abuse, and this added abuse that happened twice a week. Sadly, I had been groomed into thinking nothing was wrong with this type of behaviour.

I thought the abuse and molestation I went through as a child were normal until I had a normal boyfriend. My normal boyfriend allowed me to experience "normal love." At the age of 15, I started to feel wrong about the molestation and it left me hating myself. I felt disgusted in comparison to when I was with my boyfriend.

I decided to leave home and thankfully, the molestation stopped. Sadly, I was left with the residue of abuse, soul ties, and in need of deliverance. I had no idea such sexual behaviour was harmful. Sex was not sacred or wrong to me. I did not know the difference between sexual abuse and sexual intimacy. I engaged in sex because I was conditioned and habitually sexually groomed. I allowed the Enemy to take legal authority over my body with sexual immorality. Every sexual encounter outside of marriage is a sin against our bodies, whether it is consensual or not.

> *I say then: Walk in the Spirit, and you shall not fulfil the lust of the flesh. For the flesh lusts against the Spirit, and the Spirit against the flesh; and these are contrary to one another so that you do not do the things that you wish. But if you are led by the Spirit, you are not under the law. Now the works of the flesh are evident, which are: adultery, fornication, uncleanness, lewdness.* (Galatians 5:16-19, NKJV)

This verse of Scripture indicates that your flesh craves what you feed it. I was ignorant of what I was feeding my flesh and became subject to the things done to my body. I became conditioned to the flesh's feelings because of what I had been subjected to since I was four years old. The Devil desires that we remain ignorant of his devices. I was dying inside because of my lack of knowledge. I was not aware of what was going on with me. *"My people are destroyed for lack of knowledge. Because you have rejected knowledge, I also will reject you from being a priest for Me; Because you have forgotten the law of your God, I also will forget your children"* (Hosea 4:6, NKJV).

Growing up, my behaviour was very sexualised. I would always get into sticky situations. During my childhood, I spent a lot of time in church and Sunday school with my mum. She would attend deliverance ministries at our local church. She was a prayer warrior and a huge part of my ongoing deliverance. It was fun at the time, but I did not know my mum was laying a foundation for my future ministry in deliverance. One of the churches we attended had an enormous deliverance ministry specialising in expelling demons and unclean spirits. I would see people being delivered from all sorts of things. One of the most powerful things I noticed was when the pastor said to some of the congregation, "Vomit and go." The people were not themselves; they vomited things and then returned the next day to testify that they were set free from whatever was tormenting them. I also received deliverance through this church.

The Enemy attempted to hijack, handicap, steal, divert, and change my destiny in many ways. But God was always a step ahead of the Devil. No matter the mess I got myself into or the wrong decisions I made, God's faithfulness and mercies always prevailed.

As you search yourself, you will find that he uses these tactics and strategies in your life too. Perhaps he is making you feel too proud to admit your wrongs. He does not want you to ask for forgiveness from your spouse, children, or others you have hurt. Maybe your relationships are strained and leading to open rebellion. You may feel too ashamed to admit your wrongs, but it is pride that is holding you back and making you justify your sins and disobedience. Once you identify sin in your life, seek mercy and forgiveness. Also, do not be ignorant of the Devil's tactic of distraction. He can throw distractions of any kind for you to make irreversible errors. And as you have read from my story, he uses what you see and hear: the movies you watch, music you listen to, magazines you read, and all the media on your phone to affect you. If what you see always has sexual appeal, you might find it difficult to shake off continuous thoughts of sex from your mind. Eventually, it will rule you. Avoid these things like a disease. Free your mind from lust and its influencers.

Idols, whether they are people, objects, or abstract things must be separated from you. Everything you idolize is demonized. In other words, a demon is behind that object, person, or thing. Invariably, this means you are serving that demon and focusing on it. God does not tolerate this. He will take a step back. Consequently, the destiny destroyer will have more room in your life. So if you have an idol in your life, tear it down and seek God consciously and continuously through His Word.

Your friends and who you spend your time with also tell a lot about who you are. So be mindful of your company. Socialise with righteous people. Avoid the company of sinners and scorners whose sole aim is to be used by the destiny destroyer to steal your destiny.

Stay alert, vigilant, and prayerful.

"Be sober, be vigilant; because your adversary the devil walks about like a roaring lion, seeking whom he may devour" (1 Peter 5:8, NKJV).

"But the end of all things is at hand; therefore, be serious and watchful in your prayers" (1 Peter 4:7, NKJV)

Prayer

Lord, thank You for keeping us during our childhood. Thank You for protecting and guiding us when we didn't even know You were there. Heavenly Father, we appreciate Your protection and guidance. We are grateful You did not allow the destiny stealer to steal our destinies. Lord, in the name of Jesus, as I write down and discover these areas that may have been stolen from my childhood, I seek You now for full recovery from the Enemy and total healing from childhood trauma. In Jesus' name, I pray. Amen.

Reflections

Think about and write down the things that happened to you in your childhood, which the Enemy tried to use to steal your destiny. Write down your experiences, memories, and trauma. Also, reflect on the areas in which God was protecting and keeping you when you didn't even realise it.

_____

_____

_____

_____

_____

_____

_____

_____

_____

_____

_____

_____

_____

_____

_____

_____

_____

_____

_____

_____

_____

_____

_____

PART TWO
THE LEGALITY OF THE DESTINY STEALER THE PROBLEM OF SIN, AND ITS INFLUENCERS

CHAPTER FOUR
REFLECTIONS

Satan always looks for an open door to enter our lives. If there are past issues our ancestors have not repented from, I can guarantee you he will use them to defame you or worse. He will have you living a lie and make you believe it's not! All the while, he will be stealing your destiny. The destiny stealer tried to use this on me but my God is incredible! No matter what is going on, He has a plan. He saved my family and me. He delivered us from all of our afflictions when we purposefully sought him! When you think of an enemy, what do you think he is trying to do all the time? Enemies try to define your character, embarrass you, discredit you, and make you feel as if you shouldn't be where you are. This is precisely what the Devil intends for us; he intimidates us to steal our destinies.

The destiny stealer is a jealous angel whom the Lord Jesus Christ had to cast out from the heavens. The Enemy despises the children of God because he hates the fact that we are made in God's image!

Human beings have lost our understanding of who we are because we are now living under human taps and practical terms as I like to call it. We no longer live by the decrees and declarations of the Bible. We live by our feelings and emotions. *"For out of the heart proceed evil thoughts, murders, adulteries, fornications, thefts, false witness, and blasphemies. These are the things which defile a man, but to eat with unwashed hands does not defile a man"* (Matthew 15:19-20, NKJV).

Our hearts and souls have been taken over by sin. We no longer suppress feelings that are unhealthy or ungodly. We embrace everything we feel, think, and believe is our right to execute. There lies the trap of the Enemy. This is one of the biggest lies he uses to contaminate our world today.

I encourage you to reflect on your life from your childhood to the present and look at the different challenges and hurt you have endured. Ponder on these areas because your destiny is essential. Once you reflect on these things, you will identify the areas where the Devil has tried to destroy or steal your future. When looking, you may also see the areas of your life you planned to work on but because of the traumatic experiences, you didn't follow through. Could this have led you to experience extreme trauma, hurt, pain, anxiety, rejection, and a variety of negative feelings? You may not have been aware that these were deliberate ploys of the Enemy to steal your destiny!

Use the blank pages at the end of this chapter to jot down what you identified. Use them as points for prayer and declarations. Also, at the end of this chapter, I want you to think, reflect, and write about all of the things the Devil has done to steal your destiny. Document all the negative things, events, or experiences that may have happened to you or your family, which stopped you from fulfilling your plans. You know best what they are. I can assure you the destiny stealer will work relentlessly with his agents to prevent you from succeeding.

Reflections

CHAPTER FIVE
LEGALITY ONE: SIN

The word "steal" means to take another person's property without legal right and any intention of returning it. The Enemy comes to steal from areas in our lives he believes he has a legal right to, where sin has been committed. You need to identify those areas where the Enemy has messed with you. Use your God-given authority and take back that legal right using prayer, declarations, and deliverance. Do this because our common enemy, the Devil, desires to destroy, ruin, and take you out spiritually and emotionally by any means necessary. And he doesn't play fair.

"A legal right is the permission or consent an evil spirit has gained in a person's life through the person's sin, generational sin, or iniquity through traumatic events, occult activity, vows or oaths, wrong beliefs, word curses, etc. These must be renounced and repented of" (Pastor Bev Tucker, *Setting the Captives Free Deliverance Manual, 2016*)

"Whosoever committeth sin transgresseth also the law: for sin is the transgression of the law" (1 John 3:4, KJV).

"For the wages of sin is death" (Romans 6:23a, KJV).

Sin is like a magnet of sorts; it attracts everything it is supposed to. Sin not only gives the Enemy the legal right to enter and operate in your life, but it also attracts the Enemy. If you know you are living in sin but refuse to repent, the presence of the Enemy will continue to rapidly multiply in your life. God's presence will dwindle. Light and darkness do not mix.

Repent immediately when you become aware you have given the Enemy a chance to enter your life through sin. Pray out the powers and influence of darkness from your life. After you have repented and started seeking God, He will draw closer to you.

God is always by your side. Live holy and continuously offer worship and praise to God. He is pleased with those who are holy and attracted to those who praise and worship Him always and in any situation. Make God the center of your life and the Devil will take a continuous leave of absence.

If the legal rights of sin remain in a person's life, he or she is unlikely to be set free. Even if some deliverance takes place without the legal rights being removed, the person will always be open to the attacks of the Enemy.

Prayer

Thank you, Abba, that I have a great Father like You who always accepts me back into His fold no matter what I have done to allow the enemy access into my life. Thank you, Savior, for dying on the cross for me and making a way that I can come back to you. I come back to you, Lord, by asking for forgiveness because when you died, you took away my sins permanently, so the enemy cannot have legal access. Lord, I thank you that I am free, thank you for blocking the destiny stealer's entry into my life. In Jesus' name, I pray. Amen

Reflections

Reflect on how often you seek God to forgive your sins or ask God to forgive sins you are unaware of that you are committing.

_____

_____

_____

_____

_____

_____

_____

_____

_____

_____

_____

_____

_____

_____

_____

_____

_____

_____

_____

_____

_____

_____

CHAPTER SIX
LEGALITY TWO GENERATIONAL CURSES AND REPEATED PATTERNS

The destiny stealer's primary job is to plant seeds of destruction, anything outside of God's will. For generations, the Enemy has been known for enforcing generational curses. Initially, I had no idea what they were or how to overcome them. But now, I do. By the end of this chapter, you will also be able to identify generational curses in your life. Generational curses are issues or problems you struggle with, which other members of your family also have problems with. By the end of the chapter, you should be able to identify these curses that have been plaguing your bloodline for many generations. For example, overeating and gluttony are tied to a generational blessing of being able to cook and bake. I've been overweight for most of my life. Many of my family members are also overweight. I used to say you can't have it all and if God had made me slim, I would have been awful. After all, we are also a very attractive family. I was arrogant. However, now, I know these were all lies from the destiny stealer. He was trying to use this to enforce the generational curse of being overweight, and for me to pass down it on to my children.

People would say to me, "You have a pretty face." However, I could tell by their faces they were ashamed of the rest of my body. For years, I went around declaring I was a pretty big girl, and God knows why He didn't make me slim. Do you see how the Devil can make you believe his curses are from God? I am big because of my heritage. I gave the Enemy legal access to continue this struggle within my life because I owned and agreed with it, instead of canceling it with the blood of Jesus who has redeemed us from the curse of the law. Our tongues and words carry power. The tongue can bring death or life; those who love to talk will reap the consequences (Proverbs 18:21, NLT). Our thoughts are just as powerful and can trigger manifestations. *"Be careful about what you are thinking. For as he thinks in his heart, so is he. "Eat and drink!" he says to you, But his heart is not with you"* (Proverbs 23:7, NKJV).

How sad it is that we unknowingly carry generational curses. We have no idea that the Enemy has deliberately caused us to believe his lies, so we can continue the curse in our bloodlines. To overcome the destiny stealer, you need to be delivered from the curses in your life. It is best to renounce them by declaring they do not belong in your bloodline anymore. You must admit there is a struggle within your bloodline. Then ask for forgiveness for yourself and on behalf of your family.

Don't go telling your family members they have issues and need to repent. No! You repent for yourself and on behalf of everyone in your family. It's a personal journey, and I encourage you to keep it that way. I also recommend that you pray your family comes to an understanding, repent, and seek deliverance for themselves. Doing this will start your liberation. You will stop those strongholds from plaguing you.

Galatians 3:13 is a good place to start. Stand on God's promises in this verse and cancel every generational curse in your life and family.

Another generational curse in my bloodline is having children out of wedlock. This is usually an indicator that the sin of fornication has taken place. I was born out of wedlock. Until recently, I believed I was a love child born as a result of adultery. However, I now understand my parents were not married to each other. My father was also not married to anyone else. God said sex is for marriage, so the sin identified is fornication. The sin of fornication (which I also committed) continued to strengthen as it is passed down the bloodline. I fornicated by having sex before marriage and was heavily pregnant when I married my son's dad. I was born out of great love; however, I have identified fornication as a repeated pattern. I committed the sin over and over again.

We are all born into a world of sin, but some sins may not be identifiable at birth, for example, being born out of wedlock. Surely, I was sinful at birth. I was sinful from the time my mother conceived me (Psalm 51:5, NIVUK). This sin would be unknown to the child because the parents committed the act. The child was just born into it; this would be considered a generational curse. A cycle that is repeated in the bloodline for generations. The Both are signs of sins committed by my parents and me. God recognises covenants and honours marriage. *"Therefore, a man shall leave his father and mother and be joined to his wife, and they shall become one flesh"* (Genesis 2:24, NKJV).

On my marriage journey with my beloved husband, I have come to understand the legalities of marriage. I understand that the first woman to be married to a man is the covenant wife. The two becoming one flesh is very important as it is a union that is extremely powerful and legalistic. There are a few grey areas with second and third marriages. However, if you are not legally married and are intimate with someone, you are fornicating; that is what God sees. I'm not judging anyone. I am far from being God. I fornicated many times before I was married, and I was molested.

God is not the author of confusion. He is a God of order. My mother was the first legal wife of my father, the first woman in covenant with my father. However, they are now divorced, and he has been happily married to my lovely sister's mother for many years now.

My actions gave the green light for the Enemy to operate in my life. Fornication opens the door to lust and perversion. Lust and perversion are sexual sins and immorality: masturbation, pornography, fornication, molestation, homosexuality, and paedophilia. These are the most common ones; however, I imagine you can name a few more!

Understanding your history is important. It is crucial to research your family background, find out what generational patterns are present, and break them. We must cancel and declare them null and void before entering marriage or having children. Prayer and deliverance must be a lifestyle because prayer moves God and crushes the Enemy. Satan does not use new tricks. He may try to reinstate the curse after deliverance, but if you are covered in prayer daily you will conquer. Make sure the Enemy does not keep you permanently bound by generational curses. My actions from my past will affect my children if I do not repent of my sins and ask God to cleanse my bloodline. The sins of our fathers and mothers do count!

Another level of deliverance began once I started to share my story. The Devil tried to steal and destroy my destiny! Deliverance is continuous. We must never stop seeking and maintaining our deliverance. I am daily declaring complete deliverance over this battle I have with weight until I see it manifested. Deliverance is like losing weight. You must make a lifestyle choice to keep it off. If you are not careful about keeping the weight off, it comes back on with more than you had before. Similarly, you can get deliverance but if you do not make keeping it off a lifestyle choice, you can slip back into your old habits. *"When an unclean spirit goes out of a man, he goes through dry places, rest; and finding none, he says, 'I will return to my house from which I came.' And when he comes, he finds it swept and put in order. Then he goes and takes with him seven other spirits more wicked than himself, and they enter and dwell there, and the last state of that man is worse than the first"* (Luke 11:24-26, NKJV).

Luke 11:24-26 (NKJV) is a classic example of how important it is to maintain your deliverance. We must ensure we are filled with the Word of God, the fruit of the Spirit, and the love of Christ. But the Holy Spirit produces this kind of fruit in our lives: love, joy, peace, patience, kindness, goodness, faithfulness, gentleness, and self-control. There is no law against these things (Galatians 5:22-23, NLT). If we don't maintain our deliverance or deem it important, it will be pointless. Satan uses this opportunity to become more powerful in our lives, and we give demons access to carry out the Enemy's assignments. I encourage you once you receive your deliverance to be conscious and meaningful about keeping it. Satan will relentlessly try to make you lose it!

Divorce was another generational curse within my family. This curse may have been present at birth; however, I am unaware of those moments. I know my paternal grandparents divorced and remarried and on my maternal side they had children out of wedlock. I have identified three-generational curses in my family that I have deliberately prayed to be cut out of my bloodline.

Just like my Saviour knew me and uniquely formed me before I was born, so did the Devil. Don't allow the destiny stealer to rob you of your destiny. Identify curses and break them off your bloodline, so that you can live freely through Christ. Speak to your parents or older family members about certain areas of your life to give you some prayer points. I encourage you to do these things respectfully and gently because not everyone is aware or want to believe these problems are spiritual. Be careful and use wisdom. You are not condemning or judging anyone. You are simply gathering information so you can deal with generational curses through prayer.

Another important point to note is that generational curses are normally enforced by demons. When they are cancelled through prayers, the demons leave; however, their marks and stains remain in our souls. For example, if a generational curse of immorality is in the family, once that curse is broken and the demon driven out, the mindset of the individual still has to change. This is another part of deliverance known as pulling down strongholds. We will consider this in the next chapter.

Prayer

Heavenly Father, anoint the lips of Your people. Give them wisdom, tact, and respect when speaking to family members about their past. Create opportunities for deep conversations and reflective moments with the older generations of the family. Leave no stone unturned, Lord, so we can identify and uproot generational strongholds. In Jesus' name. Amen

Reflections

Write down generational strongholds you have identified in your life while reading this chapter.

_____

_____

_____

_____

_____

_____

_____

_____

_____

_____

_____

_____

_____

_____

_____

_____

_____

_____

_____

_____

_____

_____

_____

_____

_____

CHAPTER SEVEN
LEGALITY THREE: STRONGHOLDS

We are human, but we don't wage war as humans do. We use God's mighty weapons, not worldly weapons, to knock down the strongholds of human reasoning and to destroy false arguments. We destroy every proud obstacle that keeps people from knowing God. We capture their rebellious thoughts and teach them to obey Christ. And after you have become fully obedient, we will punish everyone who remains disobedient. (2 Corinthians 10:3-6, NLT)

What are strongholds? Strongholds are thoughts, ideas, belief systems, myths, stories, concepts, ways of doing things, teachings, arguments, and everything that influences our minds but are contrary to the will of God.

In the previous chapter, I noted that every curse is enforced by a demon who affects the mentality of the person. When that curse is broken, the demon leaves, but that person's mentality remains as it was. That is a stronghold, which must be pulled down by the Word of God.

When a sinner repents of his sins, the Devil loses his grip on his life, but his mentality stays the same. As long as that person continues to dwell on his former thoughts the Devil is bound to return. This is yet another legal way the destiny destroyer steals from us. Our thoughts invite him. Therefore, Paul said, *"Don't copy the behavior and customs of this world, but let God transform you into a new person by changing the way you think. Then you will learn to know God's will for you, which is good and pleasing and perfect"* (Romans 12:2, NLT).

Seek spiritual deliverance for your soul by engaging and renewing it constantly with God's Word.

Only God's Word can pull down these demonic strongholds we have become accustomed to. Certain things you have identified to be wrong in your life may be more difficult to change or remove in your own strength. You may find yourself struggling with your thoughts, while your actual desire is for something else.

Most times, we don't even realise strongholds are in our lives because of what society deems acceptable. We become immune to immortality and lose consciousness of sin. We speak word curses over ourselves by saying things like, "It's in our family genes." This is a lie used to keep us ensnared or to undo all the deliverance God has bought for us. Hence, in my family, I have declared that all generational curses and strongholds stop with me! In Jesus' name. You should do the same.

If you are sick, a stronghold in your life will tell you it's normal to be sick. However, the Word of God speaks differently (Exodus 15:26). When you commit immorality, it's a stronghold that tells you everything is fine; everybody does it. When you do something abnormal, it's a stronghold that makes it normal in the eyes of society.

A stronghold takes you away from the Word of God and opens doors for the destiny stealer to grab what God has for you. The Word of God is your sure weapon to defeat the Enemy. You must become acquainted with God's words and use them to replace every lie the Devil and society have fed you as you grow up.

Prayer

In the name of Jesus, Father, I ask You to bring to my memory things that have happened in my past, which I need to remember to seek my future cleansing and deliverance. Lord, give me the wisdom, words, and tact to speak to family members, so I can find out family history. Such knowledge will help identify generational patterns within my bloodline, so I can destroy and stop the destiny stealer from stealing my destiny and that of future generations. In Jesus' name. Amen.

Reflections

Write down negative things, events, or experiences that may have happened to you or your family. Things that may have stopped you from fulfilling your purpose or doing a task you know should've been completed.

_____

_____

_____

_____

_____

_____

_____

_____

_____

_____

_____

_____

_____

_____

_____

_____

_____

_____

_____

_____

_____

_____

_____

PART THREE

EXPERIENCING GOD

CHAPTER EIGHT
A TRIP DOWNHILL: EFFECTS AND CAUSES OF THE DESTINY STEALERS ANTICS: A SURE PATH TO GOD'S MERCIES

AGE 16-22: THE WONDER YEARS

Leaving home at 16 years old was a decision I made to live with my boyfriend. This boyfriend made me realise that my years of molestation and abuse were not normal. The relationship went downhill quickly after we moved in together. My period stopped, so of course, I thought I was pregnant. My mum managed to contact my dad to tell him that I had left home. My dad was not in contact with my family, so I was delighted when he turned up one day outside of my workplace. He came to where I was staying and started to build a relationship with me. I still hadn't had a period, so I told my dad about my situation as I didn't want to go back home to my mum and face discipline. I also wanted to be far away from my ex-boyfriend's house. I hoped my dad would take me. He said to give him a while, and he would get back to me. About a month later, he returned and told me I could stay with him.

My "good" things in life were coming to an end. My money was drying up, and the relationship I left home for at 16 became strained. Troubles and trials began. The need for God in my life became very apparent as I started to experience more problems. I knew I needed God to show up for me, and thankfully, He did. I remember walking down the road where I lived with my ex. I had no money or food. At the time, I smoked, and I didn't even have enough money to get cigarettes. I was sad and determined not to go back home. I was walking down the road saying, "I'm sorry, Lord. I need you right now. Please help me." He answered immediately because as I walked past the newsagent I stepped on a brand-new £5 note. I rejoiced! God answered my prayer that quickly. I was able to buy cigarettes and food until I got paid. I was genuinely grateful to God.

It came to the point that my conscience was stirred, and I began to feel the burden of the lifestyle I was living. I could sense God saying to me, "Daughter, this is not the life I had intended for you." I was smoking, drinking, and partying, not wanting to change my ways. I then struggled to sleep. My ways began to lay heavy on me. I knew I couldn't go on living life my way. I wanted to live God's way and make up for lost time with Him, but I didn't know how. At this point in my life, the destiny stealer had me believing that I was not worthy of forgiveness because of all the sins I had committed. I reflected on my childhood and realised how awful it was. I also became grateful and overwhelmed because I had survived so much.

The hurt and pain I inflicted on my mum weighed heavily on my heart. Our relationship was fractured during this time, understandably so. In essence, I moved in with the other woman, which was my father's wife. Regardless if what I did was correct or not, I know my mum was hurt by my actions. I was seen as an outside child. I didn't understand at the time that my presence highlighted my dad's infidelities. I wasn't mistreated. I wasn't ill-treated at all by him or his wife. Although there was discomfort because the hurt inflicted on my mum weighed heavily on me. I just wanted my own space, especially because I thought I was pregnant. I didn't want to cause tension in my mum's house. I didn't want to go home. I wanted freedom.

I was genuinely unaware of how much my spirit and soul were being contaminated by these relationships. I was picking up spirits through fornication (having sex before marriage), and they were infecting my spirit man. Plus, I had developed soul ties through molestation. I did not know about or understand deliverance. I had not renounced or repented of any of these sins committed knowingly or unknowingly. I just continued being ignorant of the devices of the Enemy. I was in denial about what I was doing to myself. This is precisely the result the destiny stealer wants.

The destiny stealer's goal is to keep the scales on our eyes and hold us in a vicious cycle of generational curses and strongholds by continually contaminating ourselves. I declare the scales are removed from your eyes now so you can be free from any ungodly soul ties, generational curses, and strongholds. In Jesus' name.

> *Ananias went his way and entered the house; and laying his hands on him, he said, "Brother Saul, the Lord Jesus, who appeared to you on the road as you came, has sent me that you may receive your sight and be filled with the*

Holy Spirit." Immediately there fell from his eyes something like scales, and he received his sight at once; and he arose and was baptized. (Acts 9:17-18, NKJV)

Shortly after arriving at my dad's house, I found out I wasn't pregnant. Thank God for that! I had a weighty period that first month at my dad's house. I did not have a confirmation of pregnancy or proof of a miscarriage but what I do know is that I bled heavily that month. After living at my dad's house, I pursued getting a room in a home. I thank God for the support my parents gave me. God kept me the whole time. I moved into a house with six rooms. I was the only female in the house. I thanked God that my room was by the front door. I had this room for a year; then I got supported housing for teenagers going through transition. When I was about 19 years old, I received government assistance for a one-bedroom flat.

I met my African boyfriend; he was the only person I had dated for more than two years up until this point. This relationship tested my faith in God on many different levels. This season of my life felt familiar, and I thought we were supposed to be together. He was also my boyfriend when I was diagnosed with having fibroids. I had always wanted to be a mother and because he was ten years older than me, his desire to be a dad was even greater. He was the only person I brought home to my mum and dad. He met my whole family. We briefly got engaged, and my mum designed the invitations. I thought he was my husband. However, God had other ideas. He kept speaking to me even if I didn't want to listen. I had an encounter with God about my smoking. I had a terrible chest infection, and the Lord told me if I stopped smoking my chest infection would get better. I listened reluctantly, and two days later, my chest was better.

My relationship with my mum improved after I started living alone. I decided to return to college to complete my school studies part-time. I was contacted by someone from my old church and was invited back to church. I attended sporadically. My friends who invited me to church prayed with me over the phone and encouraged me to return to God fully. My conscience always troubled me about the wrong things I was doing. I still had a little prick in the back of my mind about sex before marriage, as well as smoking.

After another bout in the hospital, I was diagnosed with fibroids. My African boyfriend told his family about the diagnosis. About a month or so after, I sensed he was becoming cold. It was a bit funny, and I didn't know why. He eventually told me that his family back in Nigeria had sent him a message saying I wasn't his wife and that he should leave me because I won't be able to have children. One day, he returned from the library with a picture of a mutilated womb full of fibroids saying our relationship was over. This led me to a very dark place. I wrestled with the Lord. I couldn't believe that this was happening. The fear of never being able to conceive was unbearable. Ever since I was a little girl, all I ever wanted to be was a mum and a teacher. I knew I could be a teacher if I studied, but the urge to teach and educate my children weighed heavily on me. The sudden diagnosis and losing my relationship made me upset.

Every disappointment is a blessing. I had no clue what the Lord had in store for me. Truth is sometimes what we believe is for us may not be. The destiny stealer likes us to believe that disappointment is God's failure. I assure you it is not. Sometimes when God tells us "no" it is for our good. When He doesn't allow us to have what we think we want, it is a form of protection and ordering our steps. *"The steps of a good man are ordered by the LORD, And He delights in his way"* (Psalm 37:23, NKJV).

During this season of disappointment, I met some fantastic people who I am still friends with to this very day. It was a really interesting time. I learnt about how your environment can tarnish your spirit if you do not know how to protect yourself in prayer. The atmosphere was very hedonistic. I tried to move on without my ex; however, we didn't move on. We were back and forth with each other. We continued to be intimate with one another until I met my first son's dad. The soul tie was made, and I needed to seek deliverance to break it. Sexual sin entangles our souls. The saying two become one is a good description of what happens when we have sexual intercourse. If the person you are intimate with suffers from depression, you could find that later in your life or at any stage, you could be dealing with the same battle.

In my wonder years, I realised that molestation and sexual experiences were not healthy; they were a part of the Enemy's plan. God is a God of order, and sexual sin is detrimental to our destinies. The Enemy uses intimacy to destroy us. It clouds our judgement. However, fornication has become normalised to the point that marriage is secondary in relationships. People no longer believe that sex is for marriage. But God gave us sex for marriage only. He instructed us in the Bible to leave our mothers and fathers and cleave to our spouses. *"Therefore, a man shall leave his father and mother and be joined to his wife, and they shall become one flesh"* (Genesis 2:24, NKJV).

Becoming one flesh in marriage is scriptural. When we do not adhere to that, we create unnecessary soul ties. Sexual sins are committed against our own bodies and ourselves. Every time we are intimate, deposits of those people's spirits are left in us and vice versa. Just imagine how many deposits we have received and passed on if we have had numerous partners. I made some poor judgement calls because of the pain, rejection and hurt from past relationships. The destiny stealer tried to take my confidence, fertility, and strength. But God had other plans. God loves us and wants us to fulfil our destinies. Even when we are not thinking about Him. He is always thinking about us. *"For I know the thoughts that I think toward you, says the LORD, thoughts of peace and not of evil, to give you a future and a hope"* (Jeremiah 29:11, NKJV).

I decided to seek help to cope with my pain—the fear of being infertile and dealing with so much rejection at the age of 19. I went back to church and attended regularly. I started praying with a group of women who were all older than me, but they embraced my maturity. I was encouraged to write a list of prayer points. I wrote six:

1. Move to a bigger property
2. Get married
3. Job promotion
4. Lose weight
5. Have children
6. Be happy

Once I wrote down these prayer points, I prayed for them daily. My relationship with God grew. I had stopped dating anyone new and only had a few sporadic experiences with my ex. I sought deliverance from my childhood trauma, as well as the back and forth relationship with my ex. During one of my music practices, I broke down in the presence of a group of women at church. They all put their hands on me and prayed for my deliverance from past trauma. They declared that I would be healed and set free from any addictions I was battling. I cried during this experience. At that moment, my deliverance started. God reacts to His Word and when we believe it, His Word manifests. Below are some Scripture verses that helped me believe I was free.

"Create in me a clean heart, O God, And renew a steadfast spirit within me" (Psalm 51:10, NKJV).

"Deliver me from the guilt of bloodshed, O God, The God of my salvation, and my tongue shall sing aloud of Your righteousness" (Psalm 51:14, NKJV).

The destiny stealer wants us to remain in the state of "I'm free," and "I feel great." He wants us to feel that way, so he can execute his next move. We must fill ourselves up with Scripture and continuous prayer after we have been cleansed and delivered. If we do not the destiny stealer will have an open field to run in. We must build a hedge of protection around our fields: our families, spouses, homes, selves, and every area of our lives. If we do not fence them with a hedge, anyone or anything will trespass on them. The Enemy will come again and again with even more spirits and demons to contaminate us and keep us ensnared. *"Be sober, be vigilant; because your adversary the devil walks*

about like a roaring lion, seeking whom he may devour"
(Peter 5:8, NKJV).

Prayer

Lord, help me to make seeking deliverance a lifestyle. Let me not get complacent once deliverance has taken place. Lord, help me to stay free by seeking You always. Holy Spirit, be my guide and helper because I cannot do this on my own. In Jesus' name, I pray. Amen.

Reflections

Think and write about seasons in your life when you were in the wilderness or aimlessly wandering through situations without clarity and purpose. What were you experiencing? Did you feel hopeless or did you realise you needed help?

_____

_____

_____

_____

_____

_____

_____

_____

_____

_____

_____

_____

_____

_____

_____

_____

_____

_____

_____

_____

_____

_____

_____

PART FOUR
THE DESTINY STEALER AND GOD'S FAITHFULNESS LESSONS FROM MY MARRIAGE

CHAPTER NINE
MY BELOVED

I met my first-born son's dad when I was 10, and he was 17. I was now 19 years old. I was working at an adventure club for children; it was at this time that he popped his head into a session to say hi to one of the parents. He noticed me. We developed a friendship and started to date. He did not press the issue of intimacy, which was unique and made me feel quite nice. I thought I was special, but he was still living with his daughter's mum. He even called me her name, once. I asked why, and he admitted it he was still in a relationship. I decided to end the relationship. I was not going to tolerate this behaviour. He would still pop into the workplace, but I would ignore him. A month later, I got a call saying he had packed his stuff, and he was coming to live with me. I questioned him and found out he was finished with his daughter's mother. He said it was over. I told him this was the final chance. He was very apologetic. He moved in with me. In my mind, I believed I was going to be my first-born son's dad's wife. I believed I could not get pregnant, but in 2002 that thought changed. My pregnancy was a blessing; although I was not married, I was determined to have my child in wedlock. Six months into my pregnancy, I found out that my first-born son's dad was still in a relationship with his daughter's mum. I forgave him, and he proposed in an over-the-top way. Leading up to the wedding was quite stressful. I had several doubts.

The church I started to attend would not marry us. In fact, one of the church members said I must send him back to his children's mother and not get married to him. I was horrified by the actions of the church members. I thought they were old-fashioned in their belief system. On the wedding day, I was 2 ½ hours late. I married my son's dad at 34 weeks pregnant, so I thought. I was bubbly and happy. Two months after the wedding, I found out my son's dad was already married.

On the actual wedding day, my first husband was confronted and was told to tell me the truth. He declined and married me anyway. I had my son four weeks later under distress. However, this was the beginning and end of our marriage; the marriage was not real. I decided to divorce silently and move on.

What should have been my honeymoon with my firstborn son's dad turned out to be a recuperation holiday in Florida with my mum and sister to visit my aunt. On this trip, I met my beloved husband, the father of my four other children. However, he always says he is the father of all my children and treats my firstborn son as his own. My son was only eight months old at the time of this trip. I was in a unique place at this point in my life. I was planning to let my hair down and have fun no matter what. A prophetic word was given to me before I left on this trip that I would meet my true love who would also have a connection to America. I heard the word but didn't hold onto it. It went over my head, and I didn't take it too seriously.

I wasn't thinking about God too much or aware of how He had me covered. I was walking around in a daze of hurt trying my best to look after my son. I'm thankful that God had my back. I may not have realized, but I tuned him out frequently. Nevertheless, no matter where we are with God, He takes care of us in ways we can only imagine. We must seek Him first:

> *Therefore, I say to you, do not worry about your life, what you will eat or what you will drink; nor about your body, what you will put on. Is not life more than food and the body more than clothing? Look at the birds of the air, for they neither sow nor reap nor gather into barns; yet your heavenly Father feeds them. Are you not of more value than they? Which of you by worrying can add one cubit to his stature? "So why do you worry about clothing? Consider the lilies of the field, how they grow: they neither toil nor spin; and yet I say to you that even Solomon in all his glory was not arrayed like one of these. Now if God so clothes the grass of the field, which today is, and tomorrow is thrown into the oven, will He not much more clothe you, O you of little faith? "Therefore, do not worry, saying, 'What shall we eat?' or 'What shall we drink?' or 'What shall we wear?' For after all these things the Gentiles seek. For your heavenly Father knows that you need all these things. But seek first the kingdom of God and His righteousness, and all these things shall be added to you. (Matthew 6:25-33, NKJV)*

On arrival at my destination, I met with my cousin, who is my age mate. I asked him to bring his friends as I wanted to meet them and have fun. I also asked him to sort me out with all the local goodies and take me to the local hotspots. I had also brought with me duty-free cigarettes and duty-free alcohol in abundance. My mum was happy to look after my son as she knew I wanted to let my hair down and what I had gone through.

One night, I got dressed up and my cousin took me out with his friends. One of them was incredibly short. I have nothing against short guys, but I am a lady who prefers men taller than me. This short friend was like a fly in your ear that you just wanted to keep swotting away; he kept on talking in my ear. I wanted him to leave me alone. On the contrary, there was a quiet guy in the corner who was with us. He did not say much to me, but I noticed he was observing me. He said nothing because he didn't want to tread on his friends' toes as they started to speak to me first. That guy in the corner is my beloved husband.

I was very bold on this holiday and told my cousin I liked this other friend. He passed on the message to him. One evening, I stayed in my hotel room whilst my mum and son were at my aunt's house. My cousin's friend came over; we drank liquor and laughed consistently. After this meet up, I was certain about my feelings for my soon-to-be husband. I nudged my cousin to find out if the feelings were mutual. My cousin set up dates for the next couple of nights. My future husband, my beloved, came to my hotel room and took me out. He was a true gentleman; he did not make any attempts to touch me or anything else. I made the first move and initiated our first kiss. I was falling head over heels in love as never before.

My beloved future husband was quite reluctant to rush into things with me; only after a few more dates did we become intimate. He was like a son to my aunt and friends with my cousin for many years. My aunt had a way of saying things that would embarrass me in front of him. I wanted the floor to open up and swallow me; I was so ashamed. We became inseparable very quickly, much to the horror of my mum. The trip started to become me and my future husband's show, and my mum was the babysitter. She soon let me know she was on a holiday as well, and she didn't come to babysit. My mum refused to babysit my son in front of my beloved, and I was quite embarrassed. I was upset but what happened next stole my heart. My future husband turned around and scooped up my son and said, "Come on. Let's go." From that minute on, my mum didn't look after the baby again. He was with us the entire time for the rest of the holiday.

Our holiday was coming to an end, so I stayed at the hotel eagerly waiting for my future husband to arrive. I waited and walked around the hotel, pushing my son in his pushchair. I saw my beloved on the expressway leading to the hotel, so I got excited. I thought he was coming to the hotel but he passed it. I spent the entire day waiting to hear from him, but he did not show up. I was distraught. I went to my aunt and asked her to drive me to the spot where he would be. My aunt took me around the corner. I started to walk up the pathway, and I saw him standing outside. He was shocked to see me and dropped something out of his hand. He took me to the side, and I asked him, "Why would you let me down?" He said my cousin had reminded him this was just a holiday. I told him, "Well, this is not a holiday thing to me." From that moment onward, he didn't let me down again, and we were inseparable.

When leaving America, he gave me a teddy bear, which said forever yours. On my return to the UK, we spoke daily for 2 to 4 hours after he finished work. I spent hundreds of pounds on phone cards, and we proceeded with our long-distance relationship. Six months later, I returned to America. It was awesome. He was an amazing dad to my son. He taught him how to walk and treated him like the son he never had. They were inseparable. Those two weeks were blissful; all we did from there was talk about our future together. I had not severed any soul ties from my past relationships or sought deliverance from my past traumas other than childhood issues. Before I continue with my story, let me say this: soul ties, trauma, and generational strongholds all came into the next chapter of my life because I had not sought deliverance and disconnection from other relationships.

Four months later, my future husband arrived in the UK, and he stayed for six months. In those six months, we had so many blessings. I was still in the flat that I lived in with my bigamist husband, and my future husband was not very happy about that. He was also adamant that if I was already married, he would not marry me because I would not be his legitimate wife according to Scripture.

After everything that had happened with my son's dad, I applied for a move to a larger property. During the six months my beloved was in the UK, we got the notification to move. This was a beautiful blessing because we could now begin to build together in our home. It was only the two of us and my son. It was a clean start.

I was excited. However, I didn't seek to cleanse my spirit, soul, body, and mind. I did not pursue any spiritual disconnection from my first marriage, sexual experiences, or childhood trauma. All of these issues I had experienced were now entering my current relationship.

We moved into a two-bedroom maisonette and began our relationship together. We planned our wedding and talked about our future together. My beloved and I had still not found a church to attend. I was still praying sporadically but not deliberately. Within these six months of the relationship, my beloved and I learned a lot about our dynamics. Having a ready-made family with my son, he had to learn quickly about fatherhood. Our son was very much a daddy's boy and enjoyed having him around full time at his young age. He didn't quite understand that this wasn't his biological father. However, we told him he had two dads as soon as he was old enough. The six months my beloved spent with me in the UK were blissful. We strengthened and deepened our relationship physically. We also meditated on Bible verses. My beloved used to read to me from his childhood Bible. I loved listening to him read. He met all of my family and they loved him. I believed he was the fulfilment of the prophetic word that my husband would be from America. He was my true love. And he came with a bonus: he was pretty handsome.

The six months on my soon-to-be husband's visa was up, and he returned to America. A month-and-half after, he booked another ticket to return to London. He brought all of his things to stay. At this time, we didn't know much about the immigration process, so when I arrived at the airport, and he wasn't there, I was devastated. All I was told was that his flight landed, and he was in processing. I left and returned home and had to go back to work as usual. I was under a lot of stress that evening. Later, I received a phone call that immigration let him out with all his stuff for 24 hours. He needed to report back to the airport for them to return him home. The officials didn't believe he was coming for two weeks. They believed he was coming to stay permanently. I knew the destiny stealer was at work. He may want to destroy your destiny; however, God is always working in the background. And we don't even know it. What happens next is a classic example of all things working together for the good of those who love him. *"And we know that all things work together for good to those who love God, to those who are called according to His purpose"* (Romans 8:28, NKJV).

The immigration officer who interviewed my beloved husband had seen all of the letters we had written to each other over the years and had great mercy on my husband. He told him, "I can see this is not a holiday; however, there is a correct way to do this. The proper way would be to apply for a Spouse Visa and then return." He was let out for the night. Can you imagine how my flesh felt? We just wanted to be together. I believe God worked for me and enabled us to do what was correct.

"A man's heart plans his way, But the LORD directs his steps" (Proverbs 16:9, NKJV).

"Direct my steps by Your word, and let no iniquity have dominion over me" (Psalm 119:133, NKJV).

So later that day, I picked up my beloved, and we spent one night together. He left all of his belongings and went back to America. God opened every door so that I could return to America in November and my husband applied for his Spouse Visa. He got permission to move back to London permanently.

It was happening at last; we were together. Our families blessed us with financial support, and my grandparents were our sponsors. That way, if we ran into hardship, they would be our supporters, not the state. I left America at the beginning of December, and my beloved arrived in London on the 22nd of December with all paperwork intact and a smooth entry into London. Little did we know that 10 years later, on that date, our fifth child, our first daughter would be born.

Our first Christmas was exciting because we were preparing for a spring wedding. We also began to practice abstinence because I didn't want to have any more children out of wedlock. This commitment was hard. In fact, it became a vicious cycle. We would abstain for two days and then be intimate nonstop for a month. Then we would go back to abstinence. This went on until we got married. I do believe the Lord upheld one of my prayers. I asked Him to keep my womb until I got married and then let it multiply. This is how I found out the importance of asking God for exactly what you want and being deliberate in your prayers. We got married and enjoyed our wedding night. The next day, my period arrived. That was the last time for many months because I was pregnant with our first child. My husband believed he could not have children, but I declared the contrary. I knew this was not the case. I did what I knew to do and that was to write a spiritual declaration prayer for my husband's seed. We repented for the fornication and then I asked the Lord to bless my husband's seed. I told the Lord that our motivation for getting married is to do what is right by Him. So just under a year after we got married, we had our first son together. And within six months, I was pregnant again with our third son. So within the next three years, we had three children under five years old and three boys at that. Stay with me in the next chapter. I will share where my marriage and children's battles began and how these problems and strife affected us greatly.

Prayer

Thank You, Lord, my heavenly Father, for Your unconditional love. Thank You, Father, for loving me even when I am unlovable. Thank You, Lord, for loving me and granting my heart's desires even when I haven't acknowledged You. Father, I thank You for all You have done, all You continue to do, and all the blessings, gifts, and life. Thank You, Lord, for my husband. Thank You, Lord, for my fruit of the womb. Thank You, Lord, for giving me a second chance. In Jesus' name, I pray. Amen.

Reflections

In what areas of your life have you been abundantly blessed but you have not thanked God? Reflect and write down the areas in your life where you have gotten your heart's desires and blessings without even realising God was blessing, keeping, and loving you. After you have written down the things in your life God has blessed you with, read the Scripture verse below and write a prayer of thanksgiving for all God has done for you. We must not allow the destiny stealer to take away our gratitude and praise to God. Our praise and gratitude keep us in good standing with Him.

> *Now it happened as He went to Jerusalem that He passed through the midst of Samaria and Galilee. Then as He entered a certain village, there met Him ten men who were lepers, who stood afar off. And they lifted up their voices and said, "Jesus, Master, have mercy on us!" So, when He saw them, He said to them, "Go, show yourselves to the priests." And so it was that as they went, they were cleansed. And one of them, when he saw that he was healed, returned, and with a loud voice glorified God, and fell down on his face at His feet, giving Him thanks. And he was a Samaritan. So Jesus answered and said, "Were there not ten cleansed? But where are the nine? Were there not any found who returned to give glory to God except this foreigner?" And He said to*

him, "Arise, go your way. Your faith has made
you well. (Luke 17:11-19, NKJV)

"Therefore by Him let us continually offer the sacrifice of
praise to God, that is, the fruit of our lips, giving thanks to
His name" (Hebrews 13:15, NKJV).

_____
_____
_____
_____
_____
_____
_____
_____
_____
_____
_____
_____
_____
_____
_____
_____
_____
_____
_____
_____
_____
_____
_____
_____

CHAPTER TEN
BATTLES

The ride was rough in my first marriage, or should I say, attempted marriage to my first son's dad. What he did to me was awful. So when my beloved came on the scene, my family was very interested in the man who came into my life. He was warned not to do any foolishness. This caused a bit of tension in our marriage because my beloved thought he was being tarnished with the same brush as my first husband. But that was not the case. My family was simply protecting me the best way they knew how. I would tell them to lighten up because, at the end of the day, I had to go home. And whatever they did, I had to deal with it. Then there was our blended family; having three children under five and both of us working full-time created major challenges. My beloved struggled being without any other family members apart from the children and me; this weighed on him heavily.

He didn't have the financial freedom he wanted. I had given up smoking by this time, and recognised the amount of money we spent on cigarettes. Hence, I became quite judgmental and resistant to smoking because I saw what it did to our money; it was like putting a lighter to it. This caused friction because when we both smoked, we found the money. My beloved developed a good friendship with one of my cousins. This was a positive thing as he had no family or male friends in London. As his friendships developed, he had a bit more freedom to do other things apart from being with the children and me. However, the pressure of our circumstances began to take its toll.

In May 2008, my beloved left the children and me. I was devastated. It was hard. Yes, we had uncomfortable moments, but I didn't expect what happened. I didn't expect my husband to leave. A friend of mine who happened to have a son in the same primary school as my eldest son invited me to her church. I was praying, but I was not connected to God as I should have been. I kept having this feeling that God wanted my attention. I wasn't attending church. I needed and secretly longed for a relationship with God. I returned to the church, but it was just a Sunday affair. Eventually, I reconnected with God. It was a relationship I did not have in a long time. It wasn't about the building; it wasn't about the people. I just sensed a presence I believed was God. By the end of May, beginning of June, I was attending a new church regularly. I am extremely grateful for New Wine International. The children and I enjoyed attending church there. I met my first mentor at their first weekend women's retreat. I bought her book, and I couldn't put it down all weekend. The book was amazing and inspirational, and I knew I would connect to her at some stage in my life. However, at this time, I was not ready to commit to an outside person's involvement in my life. I was not prepared for accountability.

I continued working on my relationship with God and attending church regularly. By September, my husband and I reconciled, and he came home. Although he came home, I was still hurting. I had not dealt with the pain I endured because when he left. I was also carrying all of my childhood pain. After a while, the cracks in my life began to show. The blended family issues were a recurring problem for our eldest son who wanted to see his biological father. I wasn't prepared when our son first asked to see his biological father. As time went on, I was warming to the idea. However, I wanted it to happen on my terms, when I was ready for them to meet. My beloved was happy to go along with what I decided, but I perceived he might have been disappointed and rejected. Still, he supported the decision. This coincided with my son's behaviour deteriorating at school; he was getting into a bit of trouble.

I thought I had completely healed from my son's dad whom I called a bigamist. He made me believe we were legitimately married when he was still married to another woman. Time helped me heal. And thank God, it didn't stop my future. If I didn't go through what I went through with my son's dad, I wouldn't have gone on holiday, and I would never have met my beloved husband.

The destiny stealer likes to operate in places where there are open wounds. He attacks areas of our lives where there is no healing, deliverance, or spiritual closure. After my husband returned, I just plodded along with my life overlooking the wounds and bruises and making no effort to heal, repent, or be delivered. I did not ask God to close any spiritual doors opened due to my behaviour. I did not ask the Lord to heal our children from the pain they experienced from our beloved leaving the family home. I just assumed they were okay and did not ask God for any assistance in parenting and caring for them. I still did everything according to my understanding instead of leaning on God or seeking the Holy Spirit. *"Trust in the LORD with all your heart and lean not on your own understanding; In all your ways acknowledge Him, And He shall direct your paths. Do not be wise in your own eyes; Fear the LORD and depart from evil"* (Proverbs 3:5-7, NKJV).

My beloved and I both worked full time and had to use before and after school childcare. Due to my eldest son's issues at school, I decided to transfer him to a school closer to home. It seemed like a good idea. However, because of what happened next, I'm not sure if it was. At this stage of my life, consulting God was still not a first priority. I acted on how I felt. I did whatever I pleased. Our second son joined our first son at the school in the new academic year, so the two of them were there together. My second son did not settle in immediately. He had many attachment issues, would cry, and have massive tantrums if he failed to get his way.

We were relatively new to the school. Perhaps that's why they did not inform me that my eldest son was having issues there as well. In the last week of the term, he came home and said that the teacher had called him scruffy because of the torn patch he had on the knee of his school uniform. She made this comment openly, and my son felt embarrassed by it. When he came home and told me this, I decided to make an appointment to see the teacher, as well as other senior staff members. At the meeting, the teacher said she acted inappropriately and was sorry for making that comment.

I expressed my annoyance calmly and explained that embarrassing my child in this manner was unacceptable, and the teacher should have come to me. I was the person responsible for buying the school uniform, not my son. The teacher was not happy that I said this and didn't say much more in the meeting, except giving an apology. The meeting ended with no sign of future problems. I was satisfied.

The school week after half term holidays, my beloved went to pick up the two eldest children. I had our youngest child with me as he attended the school I worked at. My beloved called me and said he could not pick up the children. Social services had been called, and they were waiting at the school with the police for me to bring our youngest child there. I was numb. I was in total shock. That morning, my eldest son had been acting up. I was extremely exhausted because my Nana was in the hospital having surgery. My mum wasn't in the country, so I supported the family by cooking dinner for Nana after work and dropping it at the hospital for her before coming home. That morning, I was extra tired and had less patience. So when my son started misbehaving, I said to him, "The way you are behaving when I'm talking to you, it's as if I am doing you something wrong. You had better be mindful of the way you're behaving and carrying on because the way you're going on, you are going to make social services take you." Did you catch that? Not even 24 hours earlier, I spoke the words from my mouth that social services could possibly take him away. *"Death and life are in the power of the tongue, and those who love it will eat its fruits"* (Proverbs 18:21, ESV).

I was eating the fruit of my tongue with no understanding at the time. I am not saying God was punishing me or that I deserved what I was getting. I am highlighting the power of what you speak to affect life situations, your body, marriage, and children. It's not a joke; it's real, and our mouths are powerful. I arrived at the school with my three-year-old, the third son. My beloved and I were taken into another room, and my three-year-old was taken to where his siblings were. I felt incensed and devastated that my son said he didn't want to come home because he was afraid. He knew he had misbehaved, and there would've been consequences for his actions. Now, when I say consequences, I didn't mean I would have beaten or hurt him, but I may have smacked him at the time. Ignorance is surely not bliss. I had taken many safeguarding courses, and I worked with families and children. However, I did not know it was illegal to use an instrument to smack your child. Any instrument could be classified as a weapon—a newspaper, belt, wooden spoon, or anything other than your hand. My son said he had been smacked and it was deemed as being hit with a belt. This meant we could have been arrested for physical abuse.

This was all very shocking to my beloved and me because we never beat our children in the way they were trying to make it out to be. However, we learnt that our terminology had put us in that position. As a child, I got smacked, and we used to call our smacks "beats." We were using the same terminology with our children incognisant of society's association of a smack with a belt buckle and abuse. Sadly, as a family, we were being made an example of. In the news, a young black girl slipped through so many agencies' hands and died due to the referrals not adding up. There was also a scandal involving a parent covering up her abuse of her child; the baby died.

With all that happening, they were not going to take my child's allegations lightly. They would not deem him as a naughty child or overlook it. Considering all the other mitigating factors, they took his word, and we were not allowed to take any of our children home that night. They told us to come to their office the next day and sign the paperwork. As I left the school's office, I cried and wailed. I was devastated. I could not believe what was happening to me. I also didn't know what to do. I remembered that my brother's partner's sister was a social worker, so we decided to seek her advice. I know now that what I did then was wrong. She suggested we sign the paperwork and allow social services to do their investigations. I didn't realise she was giving me advice from a social worker's point of view, not as parents who were wrongly accused of abusing their children.

We were scared. Our three children were away from us with no contact whatsoever. All we wanted to do was get them back, and we were prepared to do anything. We had no understanding of the law at this time. We just did what we were told to do and that was to sign the papers. On the third day of our children's absence, I received a letter in the post. A few months before that, I had applied for a larger property. We had an offer for a brand-new, three-bedroom house. I was ecstatic! It felt like a glimmer of hope and that God was in complete control of this situation. What the Enemy had planned for evil was going to work out for our good, even if I couldn't see it during this difficult time.

My workplace was supportive and approved paid leave for me to sort my situation out. It was evident the destiny stealer was trying to steal my family, reputation, and mind. The family I had desired so much was not with me. My husband was furious and hurt. I did not know how to make the situation right. Our dog had also gone missing a week before the children left. I felt hopeless. My children were gone; my dog was gone; everything was gone.

I spoke to a woman of God who imparted the fire of the Holy Spirit into my belly. She declared who I was in Christ and the authority I carried. She also gave me instructions to fast and pray, as well as say declarations to command my situation to turn around. I can't remember the Scripture verses she gave me, but I used them, slept in the boys' room, fasted, prayed, and believed in God. I believed God for amazing things; one was to bring my children home. My church was also tremendous and gave me and my beloved an enormous amount of support. My mum, dad, siblings, and family were also very supportive during this time. We were so grateful for their support.

I don't know how I survived. What I do know is that my faith grew because of this situation. Every crisis I overcame caused my faith to grow more and more. The more situations God got me through, the more I realised He is the Author and Finisher of my life. *"Looking unto Jesus, the author and finisher of our faith, who for the joy that was set before Him endured the cross, despising the shame, and has sat down at the right hand of the throne of God"* (Hebrews 12:2, NKJV).

By signing the Section 20 form we consented to the local authorities taking our children into voluntary care. As a result, this slowed down their investigations of my family. If I had not signed this paperwork, they would have had 72 hours to conclude everything they needed to do and return the children to my care. They would have had to go to court for a care order. But my ignorance showed. I tell you all this to remind you of the importance of knowing the law of the land you live in. It is paramount.

The destiny stealer will use any weakness you have to take away your identity and then brand you with his. Satan wanted to label us as abusers and bad, neglectful parents. I believed I was doing all I needed to teach my child right from wrong by chastising him when he needed correction. But he desired to see his biological father and was using the situation to get that.

After ten long days of not having any contact with our children, we finally had a brief visit with them. I can only describe the pain as having your heart cut out and being trampled on. When I had to say goodbye, my legs buckled, and I couldn't stop screaming. The children told me hearing me cry like that was distressing for them. However, I could not see the despair on their faces.

I had spoken to a lawyer who goes to our church. She had written a letter to the council saying they reviewed the file and if there was no evidence to suggest imminent danger, the children should be returned to their parents immediately. This letter speeded up the process and a few days after we were brought in for questioning at the local police station.

I felt like a criminal. We were read our rights and interviewed. After what felt like a lifetime, my beloved and I were released with a caution. On day 17, I received a call from the local dog pound; they had found my dog. However, she looked so different; she was emaciated. She was extremely hungry and traumatised. The dog was an example of how my children were coming back home to us.

Whilst my eldest child was away from us with his siblings, he made a similar accusation about a member of the dinner staff at school. He made the allegations because they wouldn't allow him to have what he wanted. He accused the staff of rubbing his piece of bread on the floor and then giving it to him to eat. I was informed of this by the social work team. I asked and hoped that the woman was suspended from her post pending investigation and not allowed to work with children. I wanted this woman to be treated how we were. The allegation turned in our favour because it showed when our son was under pressure, he would not tell the truth. He would do this if he felt he wasn't going to get something he was looking forward to. He would also say or do things to ultimately get what he wanted. The subject matter was no longer an issue of abuse. It became an issue of identifying his needs. As parents, we had to review our parenting style, the long work hours, my son needing to see his biological father, and healing from this trauma.

On Day 20, our children came home. They had mixed emotions. I was terrified of how my beloved would react toward our eldest, but I was extremely grateful that my children were at home. Over the next few days and weeks, I had to talk with the children and try to unravel what they had gone through when they were away from us. We found out that they missed us tremendously, to the point that they tried to escape many times at night but got caught. We did not see our children when they were away unless it was a scheduled visit, so the news of their shenanigans was heart wrenching. Our children were traumatised; they were fearful and nervous about how we would react toward them. However, my husband and I embraced them and worked on how we could move forward. We went to church regularly, and we started to read the Word of God together. The Word became the foundation in every area of their lives. The Lord supported us, and our prayers were answered miraculously during this season.

It is unusual for those unaware of the social service system to get their children back in 20 days. It usually takes much longer than that. Everyone who heard what happened with our children said it was an injustice. However, we learnt a lot of things about ourselves as a family. I have also come to realise that God was setting me up to meet people and be in certain places that would eventually bless us. It didn't make the process any less painful, but glory to God, we overcame and pushed through. We reunited as a family but still needed to seek deliverance and complete healing from the trauma. The destiny stealer tried to destroy my family, but his plans to do so brought us closer together. Trust was destroyed through this process, but I thank God it can be rebuilt. We set boundaries in our house and spoke about what was best for our family.

This situation ruined my reputation. It was in tatters. I was fighting to keep my job and felt very weary. I had gotten this job the previous year by God's divine intervention. God provided help at the 11th hour. A case was brought against me declaring I was unfit for my job. A representative showed up minutes before the meeting to support my case. No one had seen him before, and he wasn't a part of my organisation. The God-given representative was excellent in his manner. He thoroughly delivered my case, and I won.

He argued I was even more qualified to do the job now because of what I had been through with social services. The panel voted unanimously in my favour, and I remained employed. To God be the glory! God fought my case, and I won; hence, my faith kept getting stronger. *"You will not need to fight in this battle. Position yourselves, stand still and see the salvation of the LORD, who is with you, O Judah and Jerusalem!' Do not fear or be dismayed; tomorrow go out against them, for the LORD is with you"* (2 Chronicles 20:17, NKJV).

It was a new beginning. We moved into a new home whilst I was fighting for my job. Two months after moving, I was pregnant for the fourth time. I believed this pregnancy was my daughter. This would be child number four. I had a new job, and my marriage had been restored for over three-and-a-half years. Our mishap seemed a distant memory.

I couldn't believe I was pregnant again. It was frowned upon by social services. They were concerned that after our experience with the children, we would get pregnant at this particular time. They believed the pregnancy would bring stress, and we might have resorted to smacking as a method of discipline. I had to trust God, no matter what was being said. I was grateful to be pregnant. *"For God has not given us a spirit of fear, but of power and of love and of a sound mind"* (2 Timothy 1:7, NKJV). I used this Scripture verse daily to move on with my life.

As life returned to normal and our children settled into a routine, clearly defined boundaries, guidelines, and consequences were established. At about four months pregnant whilst at church, a friend of mine walked past me, noticed my growing bump, and said to me, "God said, 'not this time but the next.'" I looked at this lady and, in my head, rejected everything she said. This friend of mine was quite sure about what she had said even though she did so quite flippantly. When I reminded her of her prophecy she said she didn't remember her exact words, but she knew the message was from God to me.

When I got this word, I immediately wanted to cancel it because I was desperate to have a daughter. At my first scan, they could not see if the baby was a boy or a girl. I started buying pink clothing in faith, believing it was a girl. At 34 weeks, the sonographer spotted one testicle. I was definitely having a boy. The confirmation was late because my son had an undescended testicle, which he had surgery for at 3 years old.

At 37 weeks pregnant, my husband and I had a blip in our marriage once again. He was disciplining our eldest son and was extremely firm with him. Sadly, I was still quite fearful of how we disciplined our children because of what had happened. I rushed upstairs, tussled with my husband, and tried to stop him from disciplining our eldest son. He was not smacking him; he was just shouting very loudly at him. I was defensive unnecessarily and grabbed him. This hurt my husband very much. It was the first time I had been physical with him, making him very angry. He did not retaliate; he just decided to leave. He returned at Christmas time, and we reconciled. On New Year's Day, I gave birth to my fourth son. He was very much loved and fitted right in with the rest of the family. However, the longing for a daughter did not go away.

The destiny stealer kept on trying to use fear to overcome me. The Devil has no new tricks; he repeatedly uses the situations he knows will make you fall. We may conquer, and he may desist for a while, but he will come again to destroy you with the same tactics. However, with God, we can overcome all things. *"No temptation has overtaken you except such as is common to man, but God is faithful, who will not allow you to be tempted beyond what you are able, but with the temptation will also make the way of escape, that you may be able to bear it"* (I Corinthians 10:13, NKJV).

My eldest son met with his biological dad and seemed more settled within the family. The rest of the children were excited about the arrival of their new baby brother. They all enjoyed having a new baby in the family home. Everything seemed quite good with them for a while. We no longer had social services on our case and after six months whilst still pregnant with my fourth son, the case was completely closed. I was relieved to have social services out of our lives. After relocating and all of the trauma, we decided to move the children to the local school for a fresh start for everyone.

The destiny stealer always has a plan to destroy and divide the family. The stories I share with you are of victory. The plans of the Enemy failed. However, we must remain watchful and sober-minded. *"Be sober-minded; be watchful. The devil, your adversary, prowls around like a roaring lion, seeking someone to devour"* (1 Peter 5:8, ESV). Was I sober-minded? Was I watchful for my family? Yes. Was I praying for my family? Was I covering my family? Was I praying for my children? No!

Once the storm had passed with the children, my vigilance and prayer started to wane, and I became comfortable again. Soon after, the cracks began to show in my life, and my beloved and I argued more frequently. Frankly, one of the reasons we argued was due to his dissatisfaction with the jobs he had. Our finances were an issue. I developed a business plan based on my experiences with children. I became passionate about educating parents. My husband and I did not know our purpose at this time, and we were quite distracted by the lack of finances.

Esau lost his birthright because he got distracted from God's assignment due to hunger. Remember, hunger is an essential part of the bodily function that we all have. Esau and Jacob were brothers; one was favoured over the other. The eldest sibling lost his birthright because he was hungry. He sold it to his younger brother just to be filled. I mention this because my husband and I were both distracted from praying and seeking our children's deliverance. After all, we focused on money and providing for our family, which left the door open for the destiny stealer to come in. You can read this story in Genesis Chapter 25. I encourage you to read this to understand what you can miss out on if you are not deliberate about what you are doing in life.

Prayer

Lord, I pray we will never become so distracted or comfortable that we stop praying. Help us to remain Christ-focused at all times. Father, I thank You for keeping us in times of trouble even when we are not looking to You. Teach us to look to You always. Lord help us to pray without ceasing and trust You to deliver us through every storm because You paid the price for our sins when You died and rose again. In Jesus' name, we pray.

Reflections

Write down areas of your life where you may have become distracted by your circumstances or events. When you are reflecting, also write about the times when you were so focused on something that it didn't occur. Think and write about the areas of your life you have focused on and what you have achieved.

CHAPTER ELEVEN
THE BEGINNING OF MARRIAGE MAYHEM

I was distracted in my relationship with God. My marriage wasn't my focus either due to family issues. There was also a feeling of satisfaction. I had all of my heart's desires and felt complete as I had finally given birth to my fifth child, a daughter, in 2014. In May 2016, my husband and I decided to go on a triple date to rekindle our passion that had simmered down due to the stress of parenting five children. The date night was with two other couples, who also understood the dynamics of marriage and wanted to socialise with other married people. The night was beautiful, and I wanted to create more time for my hubby and me. Truthfully, the lack of prayer time and time with God was becoming more evident, even though I was attending church every Sunday.

Within my marriage, my beloved and I had a mutual understanding of intimacy. I believed you must give your body to your husband no matter what. It didn't matter if I was nine months pregnant. I always gave my body to my husband. I could be vexed or happy; it was the standard that we were always intimate. However, I thought I lacked love and affection, which is why we created a date night. I felt we may be intimate all the time, but I needed compliments and affection from my husband. I also believed frequent sex would be a foolproof plan to ensure my beloved husband would never stray outside of our marriage. So, if I gave my body, he wouldn't look for sex outside our marriage. But I learned that everything we do in the flesh cannot outdo the spiritual realm. We need to always tap into the spiritual world to do the things we need to do in the flesh. I was trying to keep my husband faithful by always giving him my body in the flesh. I truly believed sex would keep him from committing adultery. I also believed he would never commit adultery because of his childhood.

He expressed that he never understood how men could have three families at once. However, he never judged anyone. He didn't understand the capability of living that type of lifestyle. My beloved husband was empathetic to some of the struggles I had endured with my siblings from my father's side just because we were different. He never disrespected or was unpleasant to my siblings. We all got along really well; however, he found it overwhelming. He expressed that this would never be his portion and was glad that he had all of his children in one place. *"I don't really understand myself, for I want to do what is right, but I don't do it. Instead, I do what I hate* (Romans 7:15, NLT). The apostle Paul speaks about how we can be ensnared by the exact things we dislike or can't imagine ourselves doing. Therefore, we must rely on God and the Holy Spirit for comfort and help on the earth because, in our own strength, we will fail!

Shortly after my triple date night experience, I was contacted via social media by a guy I had a brief encounter with. I told my beloved he had contacted me, and he was okay with him being on my social media platforms. I enjoyed the attention the man gave to me. He was very complimentary. As I mentioned before, my beloved wasn't very forthcoming with the compliments; however, he always made me feel beautiful. I just wanted his feelings to be voiced. I began to look forward to this man's messages. I was giving him attention because I had not severed the soul ties between us many years prior.

I learnt about severing soul ties in one of my sessions with my UK mentor. When I was praying for my daughter, one of the areas that my mentor suggested we tackle first was my past. I was given the assignment to untangle myself from past relationships, whether appropriate or not. My mentor taught me that ungodly soul ties to anyone I had been intimate with or had a soul tie to could cause a delay in receiving what we were praying for. Many years prior, I made a confession that my daughter would not experience the things I had gone through as a child. I had to align my prayers with the Word of God and disconnect from every ungodly soul tie from my past.

I called out by name everyone I had been intimate with and disconnected from them spiritually and physically. I did this by asking for forgiveness for the sin of fornication. I renounced the spirit of lust and perversion in my life and denied their legal access through childhood molestation and generational sin. I asked the Lord to disconnect me from any spirit that was not of him and anyone who was still connected to my spirit to be removed instantly. All ungodly emotions they may have held for me in their hearts were being released and severed permanently in the name of Jesus. It is crucial to sever any soul ties that hinder your destiny. I had totally forgotten that I had not disconnected from this one person from my past.

I blanked out an embarrassing situation that happened when I had an encounter with him. While staying with my mum to recoup from the trauma I experienced with my first son's dad, I bumped into this person roughly after a week of being there. When I returned to my mum's house, I invited him over for dinner, as I do love to cook. I had minimal contact with my son's dad due to what happened between us. There was just the occasional phone call, so I was surprised on the day I invited this guy over that I had an encounter with my son's dad. He came to my house unexpectedly. To say he was furious was an understatement. He saw me entertaining another man in his son's presence. He kicked off and started to threaten me. He even told the guy they could join forces and beat me together. The guy left, and I never heard from him again. I had completely forgotten about that moment because I was so embarrassed and hurt I didn't want to remember.

In 2016, when this guy contacted me on Facebook, he reminded me of what had happened. I only remembered that he had rejected me because I was 16, and he felt that the age gap was too big. I blanked out what happened. This is an excellent example of why it is vital to pray and ask God to bring to remembrance deep hidden memories within our minds. The Enemy can use past hidden things to cause situations to occur later on in life if they haven't been dealt with in the spiritual realm.

The destiny stealer likes us to forget so he can create havoc at a later stage in our lives. It is important to quickly repent, renounce, repair, and reconcile to God to prevent situations from escalating in the spiritual realm. I was enjoying this man's attention, not aware of the soul ties. I was entertaining him with the belief that it was innocent. Around the same time, a woman contacted my husband on social media.

My conscience and the pull from the Holy Spirit wouldn't allow me to keep up with this friendship. I noticed a pattern and realised it was the Enemy at work. Every single time I had a cross word with my beloved husband, the guy would message me on social media. It was an attack from the Enemy for me to sabotage my marriage.

We are very good at blaming the Enemy for everything that goes wrong in our lives. However, we must take some responsibility because we open doors for him to enter our lives, and our actions grant him legal access to come in. I considered what I was doing and reduced our communications online.

I noticed a change in our marriage. My husband stopped being as interested in me intimately as he used to. I panicked because he is an intense guy in this area. I had also learnt from my past relationships when a guy started to play away, he naturally stopped having sex with me as frequently. My suspicions were aroused.

Being mentored was going exceptionally well, so I didn't confront my husband. I began to pray and seek forgiveness for my indulging conversations with this guy. I asked God to rekindle my flame for my husband and to help me fall back in love with him like when we first met. I also ordered a book about praying for the cheating husband. I woke early for seven days and prayed these prayers for my husband. I quickly saw a shift in his behaviour and guess what I did? Yes! I stopped praying. After this, I had a very disturbing dream that my husband was in a strip club in America receiving a lap dance from a woman. I dismissed it because I had watched a movie that was very similar and thought it was just playing over in my dreams.

My husband decided he wanted to go to America for Thanksgiving that year, and he wanted to take our daughter. To be honest, we could not have afforded to go as a whole family at that time. He wanted the family to meet our baby girl as they had already met the rest of the children. I listened to family members who said they would never allow anyone to take their children out of the country by themselves. I listened, and I did not let him take our daughter. My husband was very disappointed that I did not trust him enough to take our daughter out of the country. To be honest, my initial reaction was to let her go. But when I shared what I was going to do, it was met with horror. After the discussion, I was convinced not to let him take her. Little did I know that this was hardening my husband's heart against me. Leading up to my husband's trip, I became unwell; I was in the hospital for a few days. He would always come to the hospital late and extremely tired, and I wondered what was going on with him at this time.

This did not stop God from working a miracle. When I was in the hospital, they found a mass in my stomach. It disappeared after a few church sisters came and prayed over me and anointed my stomach. The doctor was amazed. The next day when I went for scans, the mass was gone. I was healed.

A friend of the family saw my husband a few days before he left for America and suggested he cancel his holiday because of this slight hiccup with my stay in the hospital. My husband replied, "She has her mother, father, brother, sister, aunt, uncle, cousin, and friends; what does she need me for?"

This statement opened my eyes to see my husband felt I did not need him. I had allowed everyone else's support of me to override my husband's. Not for a second am I saying I didn't appreciate my family and friends' help. I truly was grateful; however, it gave my husband the impression that I was "okay" without him. I need my husband; all wives need their husbands. Due to me not understanding my role as a helpmeet, I judged my husband based on the amount of money he provided. I didn't value his voice, and I should have no matter how much money he brought home. This showed my immaturity and incorrect mindset of marriage. Sadly, that was the way it was; due to his weakness, I did not value his opinion.

The night that my husband left to go on holiday, my mum was staying with me, she was helping me with the children after my stay in the hospital. That night, I literally forced myself onto my husband. Eventually, he gave in and made love to me. I dropped him off at the station, and he left. I remember praying and being very anxious the whole time he was away. I had knots in my stomach, and I couldn't eat. I just had the feeling that something terrible was going to happen. Two weeks passed, which seemed like forever. On his arrival back, we picked him up from the airport. He kissed me on the cheek. The only way to describe the kiss was Judas kissing Jesus on the cheek when he was about to betray Him. What is this? I wondered.

On the journey home, the music I was playing seemed to be triggering my beloved husband's emotions. Whilst we were excitedly chatting, welcoming him home, I turned and noticed he was silently crying. He had streams of tears rolling down his face. I thought this was quite weird, but I didn't overthink it. I was so excited to see him. Nothing could have prepared me for what was about to come. On our return home, my mum was there, so we carried on as usual.

Whilst my mum was helping me iron my outfit for a christening I was going to attend, I went upstairs and heard my husband on the phone. I asked, "Who is that, babe?"

He replied, "Don't ask me who is on my phone." That statement hit me like a slap in the face. His whole demeanour showed me it was a woman. After that phone call, I asked him what was going on. He shut the door, sat me down, and said, "I'm not happy. I can't stay like this anymore. I want us to separate." He said he wouldn't move out immediately. He would spend Christmas and the New Year with us, but he would leave after that. This was the beginning of the hardest two years of my life.

Prayers

Heavenly Father, forgive us for allowing our emotions to cloud our spiritual discernment. Help us, Lord, to discern the times and seasons we are in, so we can pray and battle from the offensive, instead of defensive. Prepare and equip us, Lord for battle. Lord, I pray that the destiny stealer will not cause us to quit, lose hope, and be defeated. Lord, I pray Your Word will be the double-edged sword that will crush and thwart the plans of the Enemy. We are victorious because You died for us. Thank You, Father because through You, we win!

Reflections

Have you dreamt, had a vision or did someone give you a prophecy? If yes, write it down. Think and write about the times the Holy Spirit gave you an indication something was going to happen.

_____

_____

_____

_____

_____

_____

_____

_____

_____

_____

_____

_____

_____

_____

_____

_____

_____

_____

_____

_____

_____

_____

_____

CHAPTER TWELVE
MARRIAGE IN CRISIS

The destiny stealer was coming for my marriage; he was coming in like a flood with confidence. Due to the generational curses, access was given. He had the right to try due to my husband's sins and mine. However, the destiny stealer did not realise that the blood of Jesus is against him and that all things work together for the good of those who love God (Romans 8:28, NLT). As believers in Christ, when the storm comes in like a flood, we need to understand and believe that nothing separates us from the love of God. *"Can anything ever separate us from Christ's love? Does it mean he no longer loves us if we have trouble or calamity, or are persecuted, or hungry, or destitute, or in danger, or threatened with death?"* (Romans 8:35, NLT).

Because nothing separates us from the love of God, we need to understand we walk in victory. We have been given the authority over situations that have been given or thrown at us. Our sins may have caused the war, but we still can overcome the destiny stealer and have the victory.

> *No, despite all these things, overwhelming victory is ours through Christ, who loved us. And I am convinced that nothing can ever separate us from God's love. Neither death nor*

life, neither angels nor demons, neither our fears for today nor our worries about tomorrow—not even the powers of hell can separate us from God's love. No power in the sky above or in the earth below—indeed, nothing in all creation will ever be able to separate us from the love of God that is revealed in Christ Jesus our Lord. (Romans 8:37-39, NLT)

The above passage of Scripture is one I relied on for two years whilst going through battles in my marriage. I had to learn to believe Jesus Christ is Lord of all, including my marriage. I had to re-educate my mind about what the Word of God says. The Word is key to overcoming the destiny stealer. One afternoon, I went to God in prayer, I said, "Lord, I give you my marriage."

The Lord said, "Don't tell anyone. I've got this!"

This is the second time I heard the audible voice of God.

I didn't tell anyone what the Lord told me. My mentor pushed me to keep praying. Her words and the Holy Spirit gave me belief and hope. God spoke through my mentor concerning my situation many times. He gave me another clear instruction, and it was to love my husband—unconditionally. I ensured our intimate connection was at the top of its game. I went into overdrive thinking I would keep my husband from leaving the family home.

We played happy family until the New Year. We went to church together and to my mum's for Christmas. We took family photos, which caused issues with his strange woman.

One thing God taught me that I want to emphasise is to be very mindful of my actions and to move with the Holy Spirit before I speak and act. My husband had still not offered any explanation for why he was leaving the family home. He was preoccupied with his phone and very secretive. I have no idea what I was thinking when I suggested my husband rent a room from a friend of the family who had recently broken up with his wife. I was not delivered from the spirit of control. Trying to take charge, I helped my husband leave the family home. He took the opportunity and left.

The pain I felt was excruciating; however, I was learning daily not to react because of it. The children were devastated. My husband told them he wasn't happy when he left. One of my sons even suggested it was my fault that he did. He implied that his dad left because I cut my hair. He said his father didn't like short hair. Then my son asked, "Why did you cut your hair, Mummy? Please grow back your hair, Mummy!"

This season was one of developed strategies, praise, and prayers. I knew what I had to do; my desire was for my marriage to be fully restored. In this season, I was learning that it was not good enough for me just to be a wife, I needed to learn how to be a helpmeet for my husband as it states in the book of Genesis. *"Then the Lord God said, "It is not good for the man to be alone. I will make a helper who is just right for him"* (Genesis 2:18, NLT). This verse of Scripture travailed in my Spirit. I wanted to be the helper God created me to be for my husband. I was distressed with my situation. I lost my appetite. I began to drink. I was a mess. In my spirit, I knew I was not giving up without a fight. I fasted and prayed. The Lord spoke to me about being intimate with my husband. He revealed to me that I was to keep our covenant and connection. Of course, the world would have told me to shut the intimacy down, but I felt in my spirit, I needed to do otherwise.

On the other hand, my spirit would not rest; there was another woman. I did some research and didn't find anything concrete. However, one day, a letter came to my house from the bank addressed to my husband. From that letter, I discovered who the woman was. I Googled the person's name, address, and phone number, and it came right up. I messaged the person. I was utterly enraged. This moment confirmed what I had suspected; a strange woman was involved in my circumstances. I behaved somewhat erratically—as a scorned woman.

The destiny stealer had almost won my mind at this point in my life; the situation was eating me up. The Enemy is a devourer, and I felt as if my mind, body, and soul were being consumed daily, along with my marriage. Yes, I was praying; however, I was still trying to save my marriage with my flesh. I would do things deliberately to cause confusion and force the attention of my husband, but it was not working. It just pushed him closer to the other woman. The man I believed would never do this to me was having an affair. I became very anxious. In my own strength, I tried to disconnect the relationship. I had to stop trying, let go, and let God. That year was a nightmare for me; my emotions were everywhere. The children's behaviour started to deteriorate at school. I was not the best parent. I had no support due to embarrassment and fear of judgement from family and friends about my decision to fight for my marriage.

In the third quarter of the year, amid my regular daily routine, I received a word from God for my sister-in-law. The Lord instructed me to tell her she needed to forgive to get a breakthrough in a particular area. I was obedient, so I called and told her what God said. During the conversation, my sister-in-law told me about a couple who had been completely restored and living the best life after some severe marital issues. The couple had overcome infidelity, violence, and extramarital children; their marriage was completely restored. Now that the wife's marriage was restored, she began giving strategies and tips on how to survive marriage struggles online. My sister-in-law gave me the lady's name, and I began to follow her intensely on social media.

My UK mentor fully supported me in contacting my first American mentor because she had not experienced marital issues to the extent that I was going through. I truly believed this was God-ordained for the next level of my walk with Christ. I called the woman of God, and we spoke for hours. I related to this woman and her story. I listened to every live video she had on social media. I purposely prayed for my husband and fought for my marriage on a new level. She gave me strategies on how to cope and what to do prayerfully in my situation.

I understood that the destiny stealer was determined to steal my marriage because it would take my focus off God and my purpose. This was the confirmation I needed. I learned how to be a helpmeet connected to God and assisted in my husband's deliverance. I began to understand the importance of prayer and fasting. My marriage situation didn't get better immediately when I first started praying. I had to shift my prayers and stance from a place of desperation to one of victory. My faith increased, and I loved my husband with a little more confidence that the breakthrough was coming. It didn't matter to me how long it took. I was going to succeed.

I stopped looking to get my husband delivered and looked to the Deliverer. I learnt about the power of sowing seeds into situations in my life. The seedtime and harvest time method kept my faith. I sowed good seeds into my marriage, so I knew I would receive a good harvest. However, I didn't know how my seed would manifest. I believed it would bear good fruit. The generational curse of adultery, lust, and perversion gained access into my marriage for the last time. I was going to see a harvest if I didn't give up. *"Whoever sows to please their flesh, from the flesh will reap destruction; whoever sows to please the Spirit, from the Spirit will reap eternal life. Let us not become weary in doing good, for at the proper time we will reap a harvest if we do not give up"* (Galatians 6:8-9, NIVUK). I had hope that my marriage would be fully restored, thanks to my second mentor.

"Sow for yourselves righteousness; Reap in mercy; Break up your fallow ground, For it is time to seek the LORD, Till He comes and rains righteousness on you" (Hosea 10:12, NKJV).

My husband would visit on occasion. I was getting my best friend back. In this season, I knew more about my husband than when he was in the family home. I would allow him to speak freely. I wouldn't even express anger, and he trusted me. I had stopped messaging the strange woman in

America. I stopped going through his phone. My husband behaved very erratically when he couldn't have me intimately. However, I gave in quite frequently; the love I have for my beloved husband is intense.

My mentor started to share another couple's journey of restoration after infidelity. This live video helped me tremendously. I was utterly blown away by this couple. I had insight into what was happening in my marriage. This couple's ministry, along with my UK mentor and my first American mentor was a great collaboration that catalysed deliverance.

Uncertain whether or not I should give my body to my husband, the Lord reminded me that withholding my body from my husband was an error. Scripture showed me that my body was not my own, and I needed to be intimate with my husband if he desired it. 1 Corinthians 7:4 states the wife does not have authority over her own body but yields it to her husband. In the same way, the husband does not have authority over his own body but yields it to his wife (NIVUK). It was vital for me to stay connected to my husband during this time, even if intimacy was the only connection. Through mentorship, I was taught to be wise when being intimate and if necessary, take precautions because of the infidelity. But I had to be obedient.

This was a spiritual battle. I had to pray differently. My prayers became authoritative declarations for my marriage. I prayed with new passion, poise, and purpose. I prayed with a deliverance mindset. I prayed with intention. The support I developed through my marital crisis was a lifeline to developing a passion for Christ. My husband was gone from the family home for over a year. I would frequently fall into depression. Nevertheless, I kept pushing. During this marriage crisis, I experienced so many other breakthroughs and testimonies that showed me my obedience to God was bearing fruit. God was teaching me to rely on him. *"And not only that but we also glory in tribulations, knowing that tribulation produces perseverance; and perseverance, character; and character, hope"* (Romans 5:3-4, NKJV).

This was my year of travel, and I needed to find accommodations and flights to Atlanta. The Lord told me to sow a seed of £500 to a prophet who had given me a prophetic word that was accurate about my situation and declared restoration. He confirmed I was a prophet and was going through my situation to help others. This was the beginning of my journey. The seed sown was a sacrifice to me. 48 hours later, I had an appointment with an organisation that offers support for people who have been out of work for years. I met with a lady from the organisation, and God told me to share my story about how I want to help families in non-violent resistance NVR. As I shared my journey and my testimony with this stranger, I had no clue this woman was the CEO of a big organisation and came from Tel Aviv, Israel. She was so impressed with the idea she immediately paid £502 for my flights and accommodation to Tel Aviv. I was blown away by God's power. Just 48 hours later, the seed I had sown was reinvested into my life, confirming God's word it was my season of travel. I always sow the amount God tells me to, and He has not failed yet. I developed a friendship with the CEO, which also helped with my career.

During my travel year, the destiny stealer tried to steal my health. However, I was prepared to declare I was healed with all I had learned in my marriage crisis. I noticed there was a jam in my bra. I pressed on my breast and blood appeared. I went to the doctor, got a breast scan, and they found that my breast duct was enlarged. They thought it was breast duct ectasia, which is inflammation of the breast duct. They said it is best to remove it to test the tissue because there could be an aggressive type of cancer. I was not moved by what I saw. I had the surgery and declared no cancer in my body. I healed great and would be headed to Tel Aviv. This all happened within a month. I was totally well, and a month later, I went to Atlanta. Glory be to God. The experiences in Tel Aviv and Atlanta were life-changing.

After my two trips, I also took my family on holiday to Spain, without my husband. I went to Israel, America, and Spain all in one year. God fulfilled His word. What made it even more beautiful was that I did this whilst going through issues with my husband. I could still cope with life. At the beginning of the marital issues, I did not see how I would've coped the next day, let alone the following year. In the latter half of 2018, I noticed my husband was coming around more often. I was treating him like the king he was becoming, not what his behaviour displayed. I had learnt to treat him like this from my US mentors. I used the same strategy for my children. It worked.

A turnaround point came when my brother-in-law visited the UK. I was unaware of why he had come, but he made it clear that his loyalty was to his brother's family, my family and his niece and nephews. He came to stay with us. This meant I saw more of my husband, and we did some nice stuff together. I wasn't aware that this was a breakthrough moment. Trusting in God in all things is paramount. I could have rejected my brother-in-law because of what his brother was doing at the time. However, I welcomed him, and we had a perfect time. This moment was very revealing for me and also ruffled some feathers with the strange women.

The Lord revealed to me that the support I had in my life at this time taught me how to overcome the crisis I was going through. The Lord graced me with powerhouses on long-suffering and endurance. The Word of God was always attached to overcoming a crisis. God is no respecter of persons. *"Then Peter opened his mouth, and said, of a truth, I perceive that God is no respecter of persons"* (Acts 10:34, KJV). I became deliberate in decreeing and declaring and not focusing on what I was seeing and dealing with. My husband did not like to hear the declarations during our crisis. He would ask me to turn it off and become annoyed. This made me smile as I knew it bothered his spirit!

My USA mentor had experienced her husband leaving the house multiple times for ten years. This alone made me humble. I had only endured two, which felt like a lifetime. I completed 121 counselling sessions during the process. I had lots of support in overcoming my marital issues. I could not have done this alone. I am grateful for family and mentors in this season of my life. God told me not to disclose certain things to my family, but everyone had a different part to play in my journey. Everyone was unique in his/her own way.

The destiny stealer enjoys confusion. *"For God is not the author of confusion but of peace, as in all the churches of the saints"* (I Corinthians 14:33, NKJV). To avoid confusion and out of respect for all the mighty people of God that I was working with, I endeavored to be respectful. Just as the Scripture verse above says, God is not the author of confusion. Therefore, when I became involved with my first US mentor, I asked my UK mentor's permission. When I wanted to share my couple mentor's broadcasts, I asked her permission before I showed the videos on my social media. Everything I went through and learned was great preparation for my husband to return home.

After my brother-in-law left the UK roughly eight weeks later, my husband began to stay at our family home 6 out of 7 days of the week. He was on what we call standby from work. He had just finished a building on a site. I was on eggshells during this season. He was there all the time. We would drop the children to school together in the morning, and then I would go to the job I was doing temporarily with the CEO who blessed me with a trip to Tel Aviv. For two weeks, my husband was taking me out daily. We had lots of nice meals; it was very romantic. I did not know at the time that this was his transition back home. I was just holding my breath and enjoying the moment. I treated him like a king. I didn't know what to expect. He didn't say what was going on, and he was still disappearing for at least one night of the week.

This behaviour continued from September to November. Then he said he was returning to America on his own. He left on the 30th of November 2018. I was praying for him not to go, but the Holy Spirit told me this was the breakthrough trip. I began to fast on the 1st of December. On the 5th of December, I turned my bed in a new position. I declared that this turnaround represented the turnaround in my marriage.

Whilst my husband was away, we spoke and FaceTimed quite a bit; he said he missed us. I was scared even to get excited about what I began to feel in my spirit. He had his birthday while he was out there, and he arrived just before our daughter's birthday. On his return, I felt a shift in his spirit. He kissed me in a way he hadn't done for a very long time. He no longer stayed at our family home six days out of the seven. He was there every day. We spent Christmas together, and he even went to church with us on New Year's Eve. By this point, I no longer spoke or mentioned anything about any strange women. I just prayed about them and continued to disconnect him from them spiritually. I prayed that soul ties would be severed directly and indirectly from him because of what he had been involved in. On the 2nd of January, he declared that he had returned home.

It was then I had to let my mentors know that after two years in the wilderness, my husband had returned home. The destiny stealer tried to take my marriage; however, what he did was ignite my passion and fire to crush him daily in prayer continuously. To top it off, my husband then finalised the prophetic word. In the year of travel, he booked a family holiday to America for Thanksgiving. I give God all the glory for what He allowed me to go through because it strengthened my faith. There was no fairytale restoration; it was very subtle and secure. Three months after returning home from our trip to Atlanta, he brought his clothes back home. When we went on our fantastic holiday later in the year, it was a rekindling for us both. It was also a time of deliverance for my husband. He had a lot of emotions about all that he had done and how much it hurt his family. The destiny stealer has lost. He failed to destroy my marriage. However, this does not mean he will stop trying. But I will be more prepared!

Prayer

Heavenly Father, merciful God, have mercy on my soul. Heal my heart and comfort my spirit, Lord. As I pass through troubled waters, Lord, I look to You as You are where my help comes from. I cry out to You as my ever-present help in times of trouble. Take away my heavy burden and give me Your light yoke. Increase my faith, Lord so that my mustard seed faith can move the mountains in my marriage or my painful situation.

Lord, I surrender my ways to Your ways. Lord, I believe; help my unbelief. Lord, the destiny stealer is a defeated foe. I will not be shaken by his tactics; I will not grow weary in well doing. I respect and honour my spouse and he/she loves and cherishes me. Give us the grace to be obedient, diligent, and strategic in this season because we have overcome by the blood of the Lamb and the word of our testimonies. In Jesus' name, we pray. Amen.

Reflections

The Scripture verses below are to encourage you in your fight, battles, and trauma. Write down your reflections about closure: how you envisage it and how it may not be. Write praise prayers with the help of the below Scripture verses.

"Dear brothers and sisters, when troubles of any kind come your way, consider it an opportunity for great joy, for you know that when your faith is tested, your endurance has a chance to grow. So, let it grow, for when your endurance is fully developed, you will be perfect and complete, needing nothing" (James 1:2-4, NLT).

"God blesses those who patiently endure testing and temptation. Afterwards, they will receive the crown of life that God has promised to those who love him" (James 1:12, NLT).

"But those who wait on the LORD Shall renew their strength; They shall mount up with wings like eagles, they shall run and not be weary, they shall walk and not faint" (Isaiah 40:31, NKJV).

"Endure suffering along with me, as a good soldier of Christ Jesus" (2 Timothy 2:3, NLT).

"We proudly tell God's other churches about your endurance and faithfulness in all the persecutions and hardships you are suffering" (2 Thessalonians 1:4, NLT).

PART FIVE
DIVINE STRATEGIES TO OVERCOME
THE ENEMY

CHAPTER THIRTEEN
THE WEAPONS

1. THE WHOLE ARMOUR OF GOD

Overcoming the destiny stealer is not a one-time thing; it is a lifestyle choice. I have decided that overcoming is a part of my lifestyle. Seeking deliverance daily is a way I continue to overcome the destiny stealer. The Bible says deliverance is the children's bread. In other words, deliverance is part of our inheritance in the manifold blessings of God. As believers, we must take this inheritance and wield it as a weapon daily to keep the destiny stealer out of our lives and families.

Let's examine the verse below:

> *Then Jesus went out from there and departed to the region of Tyre and Sidon. And behold, a woman of Canaan came from that region and cried out to Him, saying, "Have mercy on me, O Lord, Son of David! My daughter is severely demon-possessed." But He answered her, not a word. And His disciples came and urged Him, saying, "Send her away, for she cries out after us." But He answered and said, "I was not sent except to the lost sheep of the house of Israel."*

Then she came and worshipped Him, saying, "Lord, help me!" But He answered and said, "It is not good to take the children's bread and throw it to the little dogs." And she said, "Yes, Lord, yet even the little dogs eat the crumbs which fall from their masters' table." Then Jesus answered and said to her, "O woman, great is your faith! Let it be to you as you desire." And her daughter was healed from that very hour. (Matthew 15:21-28, NKJV)

Deliverance is the removal of unclean spirits from within us. Deliverance is a continuous thing; it's not something you do once and you're forever delivered. No! It doesn't work like that. We must consistently ask God to show us what we need to be delivered from. We must ask Him to reveal to us the areas that need to be cleaned. Whatever spirit we give access to will have the right to operate in our lives. Access happens when we open doors that should be closed. Access could happen through doors that we consciously open and doors that have been opened through generational curses. Often, we open doors knowing we shouldn't do a certain thing but do it anyway without considering the consequences of our actions. We have to be careful about what we allow into our spirits: music, movies, books we read, the people we hang around and are intimate with. Because of this, we must always seek deliverance. I recommend these books to help you through the process:

1. *Pigs in the Parlor*
2. *Set Free and Delivered*
3. *Setting the Captives Free Deliverance Manual*

154

These books are trusted aids to take us through the deliverance process. Connect with someone you trust who uses the wisdom of God in these areas to assist you.

I faced battles even before I was born. I am aware of my spiritual and fleshly battles. The destiny stealer was trying to steal my destiny from the beginning. The Bible tells us in Ephesians 6:12 (KJV), *"For we wrestle not against flesh and blood, but against principalities, against powers, against the rulers of the darkness of this world, against spiritual wickedness in high places."* The verse exposes our enemy; we must be aware of who he is and be equipped to fight. The full armour of God is an essential tool to overcoming the assignment of the destiny stealer once you have experienced deliverance. Deliverance is a cleansing process. Think about this: when we shower, we don't put on dirty clothes; we put on clean clothes. Once we are delivered, we put on the full armour of God to stay clean and aware of the destiny stealer's tactics. We have to protect our deliverance and don't allow unclean spirits to make us dirty again. We need to be ready and stay equipped for the next round. Please put on your armour. You can't live without it.

> *Finally, my brethren, be strong in the Lord and in the power of His might. Put on the whole armour of God, that you may be able to stand against the wiles of the devil, for we do not wrestle against flesh and blood, but against principalities, against powers, against the rulers of the darkness of this age, against spiritual hosts of wickedness in the heavenly places. Therefore, take up the whole armour of*

155

God, that you may be able to withstand in the evil day, and having done all, to stand. Stand therefore, having girded your waist with truth, having put on the breastplate of righteousness, and having shod your feet with the preparation of the gospel of peace; above all, taking the shield of faith with which you will be able to quench all the fiery darts of the wicked one. And take the Helmet of salvation, and the sword of the Spirit, which is the word of God; praying always with all prayer and supplication in the Spirit, being watchful to this end with all perseverance and supplication for all the saints. (Ephesians 6:10-18, NKJV)

I want to stay clean, and I encourage you to do the same. I want to stay delivered and protected from the tricks of the Enemy. I highly recommend we put on the full armour of God, at least, once a day. But, of course, more is better. Make it a priority to start your day by putting on the full armour of God.

THE ARMOUR OF GOD EXPLAINED

Helmet of Salvation: The helmet of salvation means you have become a partaker of the salvation that comes to us by grace through faith. It means being a partaker of that salvation. Your head is covered with a very special weapon. This weapon of salvation is crucial, and you must always be on guard to ensure it is not lost to sin.

Belt of Truth: Integrity is a big word with God. We are who we are and can call God faithful because of His integrity. He expects all who profess to be His children to have integrity. This factor of speaking the truth and keeping your every word earns you the approval of God and keeps the Devil away from you. When you speak lies and act deceitfully, the Devil picks it up and uses it against you (Psalm 24:4, 15:4, Ecclesiastics 5:5,6)

Breastplate of Righteousness: Righteousness means right standing with God. Once you are in right standing with God, the Devil cannot penetrate you. He knows if he tries, God will arise and defend you. So your actions must always reflect the righteousness of God, not man or society. This way, God will always be on your side. However, if your righteousness is according to society's standards, it will oppose God, and the Enemy will use this.

Shield of Faith: The Devil works mainly through fear, doubts, discouragements, disappointments, and negative emotions—something faith alone can defend. These factors mentioned are all darts the Enemy fires to weaken your resolve. However, when you have unswerving faith in God and His Word, the shield of faith will work for you.

Sword of the Spirit: The sword of the Spirit is the Word of God; you must wield it confidently and use it to cut down demonic forces and their weapons. The Word of God must flow from your mouth and your heart. It must also be used to pull down all the antics of the Devil.

Gospel of Peace: The gospel is a message of peace that should be reflected in your attitude and words. That's why Scripture says *"Follow peace with all men, and holiness, without which no man shall see the Lord"* (Hebrews 12:14).

Being a messenger of peace averts lots of trouble. Keep your mouth from speaking evil and concentrate on speaking peaceful words about the gospel of Christ.

The Whole Armour of God Declarations

- Thank You, Father, for the helmet of salvation.
- Thank You, I have salvation.
- My mind is renewed; my mind is now transformed.
- Lord, thank You for giving me the mind of Christ.
- Thank You for the Spirit of power and a sound mind.
- Thank You, Father, for protecting my sound mind with the helmet of salvation.
- Lord, guard my heart.
- Thank You, God, for guarding my heart.
- Thank You, Lord, for covering my heart with the breastplate of righteousness.
- Thank you, Lord, God, for girding my waist with truth.
- I speak death to strongholds and generational curses.
- I speak life to generations of blessings and breakthroughs in my life from this day forth.
- I pick up the double-edged sword, the Word of God that is strong enough to sever the soul from Spirit.
- I use the Word of God to crush, annihilate and thwart every plan of the Enemy for my life, my husband's life or my children's lives. In the mighty name of Jesus.
- I go under the shield of faith.
- I am protected underneath the wings of my God.
- I position my shield of faith ready to defend my family, children, priest, prophet, and king from every fiery dart of the Enemy

- No weapon fashioned against my family will prosper. In Jesus' name.
- Thank You, Father, for holding my feet with the gospel of peace.
- I declare that I walk in victory, knowing I have peace that surpasses all understanding.
- I crush and trample serpents; I tread on scorpions, and no harm will come to me because of the authority I carry in Christ Jesus.
- Thank you, Father, for the full armour of God. I put great emphasis on putting on the full armour of God. It is much needed daily.

2. PRAYERS AND STANDING ON GOD'S PROMISES

My mentors imparted to me a deeper understanding of the Scriptures and the importance of them in deliverance. Once we can understand and grasp that we are fighting a war against the unseen, we learn how to pray against strongholds, familiar spirits, and generational curses. Their access needs to be removed from our lives.

My journey to deliverance in my marriage and life involved lots of prayer and developing a closer relationship with God. I also needed to understand that the Holy Spirit was within me. I tapped into the frequency of God. I prayed that my ears would be unplugged. I fasted in many forms, including only using water for a specific time and the Daniel Fast. I prayed in the Spirit. One of the greatest strategies I learned was praying the Scriptures back to God, understanding that the Lord is moved by His Word pertaining to my situation. I prayed that my husband would love me like Christ loved the church.

Husbands, love your wives, just as Christ also loved the church and gave Himself for her, that He might sanctify and cleanse her with the washing of water by the word, that He might present her to Himself a glorious church, not having spot or wrinkle or any such thing, but that she should be holy and without blemish. (Ephesians 5:25-27, NKJV)

I prayed that only *my* breast would satisfy my husband: *"Let your fountain be blessed, and rejoice with the wife of your youth. As a loving deer and a graceful doe, Let her breasts satisfy you at all times; And always be enraptured with her love"* (Proverbs 5:18-19, NKJV).

I prayed these types of prayers for my marriage and husband. I began to see the fruit of what I prayed. God is a restorer. He restored my life. He has restored my marriage and the relationship I have with Him.

I now know that I am in tune with the Holy Spirit to hear His voice at all times for guidance on my journey with Him. I understand I am called to be an intercessor, to pray for the nations. However, my heart remains with families and marriages. I seek deliverance at all times to ensure nothing has entered me without me knowing. I am also always asking God to create in me a clean heart and renew a steadfast spirit within me (Psalm 51:10-11, NKJV).

To stay delivered and overcome the destiny stealer, I pray deliberately daily. I seek God's face in prayer. I worship the Lord in Spirit and truth. To remain clean, I understand that deliverance is a lifestyle, not a one-time experience. To remain cleansed, I pray in tongues, and I am watchful.

I walk in the Spirit, not according to my flesh. I believe we can all be overcomers! I am more than a conqueror. I am an overcomer by the blood of the Lamb and the word of my testimony. Revelation Chapter 12 keeps me focused on what the destiny stealer wants from me. However, I know and continue to seek and learn how to train my fingers to fight and my hands for war. *"Blessed be the LORD my Rock, Who trains my hands for war, And my fingers for battle— My lovingkindness and my fortress, My high tower and my deliverer, My shield and the One in whom I take refuge, Who subdues my people under me"* (Psalm 144:1-2, NKJV). I understand I am in spiritual warfare because of what I have overcome. Christ died for me to overcome, so now I say confidently, I am more than a conqueror. I am an overcomer!

> *Now a great sign appeared in heaven: a woman clothed with the sun, with the moon under her feet, and on her head a garland of twelve stars. Then being with Child, she cried out in labour and in pain to give birth. And another sign appeared in heaven: behold, a great, fiery red dragon having seven heads and ten horns, and seven diadems on his heads. His tail drew a third of the stars of heaven and threw them to the earth. And the dragon stood before the woman who was ready to give birth, to devour her Child as soon as it was born. She bore a male Child who was to rule all nations with a rod of iron. And her Child was caught up to God and His throne. Then the woman fled into the*

wilderness, where she has a place prepared by God, that they should feed her there one thousand two hundred and sixty days. And war broke out in heaven: Michael and his angels fought with the dragon, and the dragon and his angels fought, but they did not prevail, nor was a place found for them in heaven any longer. So, the great dragon was cast out, that serpent of old called the Devil and Satan, who deceives the whole world; he was cast to the earth, and his angels were cast out with him. Then I heard a loud voice saying in heaven, "Now salvation, and strength, and the kingdom of our God, and the power of His Christ have come, for the accuser of our brethren, who accused them before our God day and night, has been cast down. And they overcame him by the blood of the Lamb and by the word of their testimony, and they did not love their lives to the death. Therefore rejoice, O heavens, and you who dwell in them! Woe to the inhabitants of the earth and the sea! For the devil has come down to you, having great wrath, because he knows that he has a short time." Now when the dragon saw that he had been cast to the earth, he persecuted the woman who gave birth to the male Child. But the woman was given two wings of a great eagle, that she might fly into the wilderness to her place, where she is nourished for a time and times and half a time, from the presence of the serpent. So, the serpent spewed water out of his mouth like a flood after the woman, that he

*might cause her to be carried away by the flood.
But the earth helped the woman, and the earth
opened its mouth and swallowed up the flood
which the dragon had spewed out of his mouth.
And the dragon was enraged with the woman,
and he went to make war with the rest of her
offspring, who keep the commandments of God
and have the testimony of Jesus Christ.*
(Revelation 12:1-17, NKJV)

3. PERSISTENCE AND PERSEVERANCE UNTIL VICTORY IS WON

Are you prepared for trials? Can you see them as possible distractions or the destiny stealer doing what he does best? The destiny stealer does not stop. He plans to destroy you at any cost. He wants your destiny. I am so passionate about sharing my story because the book of Revelation says Christ has overcome the world. Therefore, no matter what you have endured, you can overcome the destiny stealer. Keep persisting. Don't give up regardless of the trials you are experiencing. As you read in my story, the destiny stealer came for my family and me time and time again. However, what I learnt changed my life. I believe you can overcome the destiny stealer, too!

How? By not giving up or allowing your situation to overwhelm you. Read your Bible. Cry out to God; pray; fast, and seek deliverance. God has your back even when you don't realise it! I pray my story helps and encourages you or someone today by sending the message of perseverance. Never give up! Continue because God will come through time and time again. That is how you overcome the destiny stealer.

"These things I have spoken to you, that in Me you may have peace. In the world you will have tribulation, but be of good cheer, I have overcome the world" (John 16:33, NKJV).

Prayer

Dear Heavenly Father, I declare that I am faithful in all my persecutions and hardship. I am suffering because I declare You are my Lord. I will use it for Your ministry and glory. Lord, I am Your good soldier who will endure to the end. I know my marriage is permanently restored. In Jesus' name. God, I believe You have blessed me by ensuring I reach the end because Your grace is sufficient for me. Those who wait on the Lord will renew their strength like eagles. Lord, my strength is renewed. I soar like an eagle. I am more than a conqueror. I am an overcomer by the blood of the Lamb and the word of my testimony. I use my experience to bless others because I trust You to see me through. Thank You, Lord, for keeping me through the storms. In Jesus' name. I pray. Amen.

Reflections

Now, using Revelation Chapter 12, write an overcomer declaration. Here is an example of mine:

- I am more than a conqueror.
- I am an overcomer because Christ died for me.
- I have overcome the war in my marriage.
- I have defeated the battle of the flesh.
- I am fit for purpose.
- I am trained and battle-ready.
- I am blessed because my Daddy is my Rock.
- My Father in heaven has given me steadfast love that never ceases.
- My prayer language is in alignment with Christ.
- I keep His commandments, and I testify of everything I have overcome. I share my testimony for God's glory, and I thank God for loving me.

Now write yours.

_____

_____

_____

_____

_____

_____

_____

_____

_____

_____

_____

CHAPTER FOURTEEN
SUKEY'S OVERCOMER NINE-STEP STRATEGY

Sukey's Overcomer Strategy is a unique nine-step tool that is used to support people who are in crises or experiencing overwhelming trauma. These nine steps are vital tools and strategies that encourage, prompt, and strengthen you to work out and overcome battles, as well as return to Christ!

O= Over and Over

The first step in being an overcomer is understanding you may have to go through trials repeatedly. Overcoming is a continuous action. You have to battle, pray, and own up to the fact you are in a crisis situation, or something is overwhelming you. By becoming an overcomer, you are identifying there is a problem. This is the start of the overcoming process. Initially, you do not know how or believe you will overcome this trial

But you will conquer to face and deal with the next situation and trials more effectively, stronger, and strategically.

V= Victory Vocabulary

Your voice and the vocabulary you use determine whether or not you will be an overcomer. Use these Victory V words for overcoming declarations.

Victory: I have won this battle, and I have the victory.

Virtuous: I have integrity, and I identify my weaknesses to turn them into strengths.

Valued: I know my worth, and God loves me.

Volume: I have the capacity to fill up with the Word of God to overcome this battle I am in.

I am capable of emptying myself of the things that are not helping me, so I can be refilled with God's Word, love, and wisdom.

These are some more victory statements:

- I have overcome my situation.
- I can do all things through Christ who strengthens me.
- The joy of the Lord is my strength.
- I look to the hills where my help comes from: the Lord, Creator of heaven and the earth.
- God's grace is sufficient for me.

E=Encourage be Encouraged

Let's evaluate your circumstances and know you are not alone. Your situation is unique; however, there is nothing new under the sun in God's eyes. *"That which has been is what will be, That which is done is what will be done, And there is nothing new under the sun"* (Ecclesiastes 1:9, NKJV). I suggest you read the entire chapter so you can be encouraged that your unique situation is quite familiar to God.

R= Responsively not Reactively

To engage and overcome your battles, you must know how to respond. When we are reactive, we usually take action without thinking about the impact. However, when we are responsive, we process the situation, consider the outcomes and think at great lengths about the impact it will have on us and others. This is similar to the flight or fight response mechanism. We do not want to act instinctively without thinking; we want to act intuitively. The best way to do this is to seek the Holy Spirit before you speak, move, or act.

C=Communication, Communion, Commitment

Your communication, communion, and commitment to God is the next step in the overcomer journey. No matter what place you are in your life, I suggest you work on your communication with Him. We communicate with God by praying to Him. In the process, we also need to listen to Him. Whilst in prayer, ask Him to speak to you or be quiet, so you can hear His instructions, directions, or Scripture. I suggest Communion for those who want to deepen their connection with Christ. Breaking bread is powerful! Commitment is essential to staying an overcomer. We must be committed to God and discipline ourselves to learn His ways. No matter what, you will need to communicate your situation, circumstance, problem, trial, or struggle to God.

Pray and tell God exactly what you are going through. Let Him know what the situation is. Do this by saying, preferably writing, or voice-noting clear, concise prayers and declarations. For example:

- Help, Lord, I am struggling with my finances.
- Jesus, I am on the verge of giving up on my marriage; show me the way.
- Heal me, Lord, and take away the pain.
- Deliver me, Lord, from my enemies.

- I need You, Lord.

Once you have communicated with God, commit to continually talking with Him no matter how hard the situation may be.

O=Obedience Is Key

Be obedient to the Word of God (the Bible).

Be obedient to the Holy Spirit. What is the Holy Spirit saying to you about your situation or destiny?

Once you have communicated with God or communed with Him, you will need to listen and obey the instructions He gives. This is paramount to overcoming and getting breakthroughs.

Obedience is better than sacrifice in this season. *"So Samuel said: "Has the LORD as great delight in burnt offerings and sacrifices, as in obeying the voice of the LORD? Behold, to obey is better than sacrifice, And to heed than the fat of rams"* (I Samuel 15:22, NKJV).

Obedience can assist you in removing obstacles. On the other hand disobedience can cause the obstacles to stay!

Detect, seek, and ask God to show you the obstacles. Let your obedience be the reason for your season.

Trials come if there is no reason for your season. As we know, we all have issues regardless.

> *Now the word of the LORD came to Samuel, saying, "I greatly regret that I have set up Saul as king, for he has turned back from following Me, and has not performed My commandments."*

And it grieved Samuel, and he cried out to the LORD all night. So when Samuel rose early in the morning to meet Saul, it was told Samuel, saying, "Saul went to Carmel, and indeed, he set up a monument for himself; and he has gone on around, passed by, and gone down to Gilgal." Then Samuel went to Saul, and Saul said to him, "Blessed, are you of the LORD! I have performed the commandment of the LORD." But Samuel said, "What then is this bleating of the sheep in my ears, and the lowing of the oxen which I hear?" And Saul said, "They have brought them from the Amalekites; for the people spared the best of the sheep and the oxen, to sacrifice to the LORD your God; and the rest we have utterly destroyed." Then Samuel said to Saul, "Be quiet! And I will tell you what the LORD said to me last night." And he said to him, "Speak on." So Samuel said, "When you were little in your own eyes, were you not head of the tribes of Israel? And did not the LORD anoint you king over Israel? Now the LORD sent you on a mission, and said, 'Go, and utterly destroy the sinners, the Amalekites, and fight against them until they are consumed.' Why then did you not obey the voice of the LORD? Why did you swoop down on the spoil, and do evil in the sight of the LORD?" And Saul said to Samuel, "But I have obeyed the voice of the LORD, and gone on the mission on which the LORD sent me, and brought back Agag king of Amalek; I have utterly destroyed the Amalekites. But the people took off the plunder, sheep and *oxen, the best of the things which should have been utterly destroyed, to sacrifice to the LORD your God in Gilgal." So Samuel said: "Has the LORD as great delight in burnt offerings and sacrifices, as in obeying the voice of the LORD? Behold, to obey is better than sacrifice, And to heed than the fat of rams.* (I Samuel 15:10-22, NKJV)

For rebellion is as the sin of witchcraft, and stubbornness is as iniquity and idolatry. Because you have rejected the word of the LORD, He also has rejected you from being king." Then Saul said to Samuel, "I have sinned, for I have transgressed the commandment of the LORD and your words because I feared the people and obeyed their voice. (I Samuel 15:23-24)

M=Meditating

Meditate on the Word of God because you are more than a conqueror. The Word of God makes sure you are grounded when stepping out in obedience. Be mindful of what you say. Pray the Scriptures back to God. Overcome your situation using your mouth as a weapon against the Enemy. *"But be doers of the word, and not hearers only, deceiving yourselves"* (James 1:22, NKJV).

E=Engage

Engage in seeking deliverance, so you are in good stead to overcome the Enemy in spiritual warfare. Prayer annihilates, crushes, and thwarts the plans of the Enemy. It equips you to overcome the destiny stealer. You have gone through deliverance and have been empowered. Now, you can focus and target your prayers to hit the bullseye every time you pray. You are empowered in your process because you are no longer afraid of it. Engaging and impacting the spiritual realm by using Scripture and the help of the Holy Spirit shift your circumstances. No matter how long it takes to manifest, be confident that the Lord has given you the victory. It's a matter of when, not if!

R=Remember

Remember what God has taken you through.

Remember what God has done for you.

Remember what God has delivered you, your spouse, or children from.

Remember that you have overcome by the blood of the Lamb and the word of your testimony.

"And they have defeated him by the blood of the Lamb and by their testimony. And they did not love their lives so much that they were afraid to die" (Revelation 12:11, NLT).

God has seen you through; now, go and write or tell your story of how you overcame. Whichever way you do it, you must record what you have overcome!

Recording what you have gone through is a good way of reminding yourself when another battle comes of all that you have already overcome. The key to overcoming is knowing you will overcome no matter what it looks like. The storm does not last forever. Your situation or battle has an end date.

You may also have to repeat a few of these steps to overcome; however, repetition is not a failure. You will overcome eventually! God's timing is not always our timing.

You overcome because of Christ. He is the victor. We overcome for His glory, not our own. Every time you overcome, make sure it is Christ you rejoice in, not yourself.

Overcoming reignites your relationship with Christ. You are an overcomer! In Jesus' name.

References

Tucker, Bev. (2016). Setting the Captives Free: Deliverance Manual. It's All About Him Media & Publishing.

About the Author

Sukaena Callander, overcomer strategist, intercessor, and emerging author, is a passionate woman of faith. She is also the CEO of S and S Global Services and the host of Sukey Saturdays and Sukey Soars. On these programmes, she shares stories, struggles, scriptures, and successes to encourage people around the world with God's faithfulness. Whilst doing this, she gives the utmost glory to God by activating keys to unlock and lock doors for His kingdom. She is a lover of Christ and will proclaim the name of Jesus around the world at any cost.

Sukaena is the wife of Shane Callander and a mother of 5: 4 boys and 1 girl. Hailing from London, UK, she has a strong passion for helping others overcome obstacles she once faced. Thus, she tells bold, life-changing stories about overcoming family issues and her son's miraculous healing from stage 4 cancer.

Sukaena is a motivated empowerment speaker with a sincere heart for seeing people overcome what they believe is impossible. Through many years of preparation, praying, and seeking the Lord for her own overcomer's strategy, she is now helping others conquer their battles.

Connect with Sukaena

Email: SandSglobalservices@gmail.com

YouTube: S&S Global Services

Facebook: S&S Global Services

Website: www.SandSglobalservice.com

Made in the USA
Columbia, SC
05 October 2023

23771743R00104